The

SUPERMARKET

for a
Meaningful Life

The
SUPERMARKET
for a
Meaningful Life

Sondra Ray
Markus Ray

Immortal Ray Productions
Nashville   Washington DC

IMMORTAL RAY PRODUCTIONS
301 TINGEY STREET SE, #338
WASHINGTON DC, 20003

immortalrayproductions@gmail.com

Immortal Ray Productions
Nashville   Washington D.C.

Library of Congress Cataloging in Publication Data

Ray, Sondra; Ray, Markus; The Supermarket for a Meaningful Life

l. Relationships 2. Life-Wisdom 3. Self-Realization

Cover Design: Immortal Ray Productions
Back Cover Image: Tajinder Chana of London

ISBN 13: Paperback 978-1-950684-12-0
ISBN 13: E-Book 978-1-950684-13-7

DEDICATION

We dedicate this book to the Dream Team. These are our main spiritual masters: Sri Herakhan Babaji, Jesus of A Course in Miracles, and Amma, a manifestation of the Divine Mother. They are the ones in our Supermarket for a Meaningful Life. We share them with the world, greatly in need of Their wisdom and meaning now.

ALSO by SONDRA RAY & MARKUS RAY

Lately I've Been Thinking II
Boundless Mercy
The Second Coming: You Are the Christ
The Perfection of Babaji
Lately I've Been Thinking
Alpha Omega
Liberation: Freedom from Your Biggest Block to Pure Joy
The Master Is Beautiful
I Deserve Love (2nd Edition)
Physical Immortality: How to Overcome Death
The New Loving Relationships Book
Babaji: My Miraculous Meetings with a Real Maha Avatar
Spiritual Intimacy: What You Really Want with a Mate
Odes to the Divine Mother
Little Ganesh Book
Liberation Breathing: The Divine Mother's Gift
Miracles with My Master, Tara Singh
Rock Your World with the Divine Mother
Pele's Wish
Healing and Holiness
The Loving Relationships Treasury
Essays on Creating Sacred Relationships
Interludes with the Gods
Inner Communion
How to Be Chic, Fabulous, and Live Forever
Pure Joy!
Birth & Relationships
Ideal Birth
Drinking the Divine
Celebration of Breath
The Only Diet There Is
Loving Relationships II
Loving Relationships I
Rebirthing in the New Age
I Deserve Love

CONTENTS:

🛒 THE SUPERMARKET

🛒 #1. AN AISLE FOR MAINTAINING JOY —1

Some people need help staying in a state of joy. These fruits are in aisle one.

🛒 #2. AN AISLE FOR ENLIGHTENMENT —14

Some people need help with enlightenment. These light bulbs are in aisle two.

🛒 #3. AN AISLE FOR ENCOURAGEMENT AND GRATITUDE —23

Some people need help with encouragement. The products for gratitude are in aisle three.

🛒 #4. AN AISLE FOR SPIRITUAL PRACTICES —28

Some people need spiritual practices. These soul foods are in aisle four.

🛒 #5. AN AISLE FOR ART & CULTURE —52

Some people need to know about art and culture to lift them out of the doldrums. These foods are in aisle five.

#6. AN AISLE FOR ENLIGHTENED BOOKS —79

Some people need enlightened books to read. We have well stocked shelves in aisle six.

#7. AN AISLE FOR SPIRITUAL MASTERS —97

Some people need a spiritual master. These masters give their wisdom in aisle seven.

#8. AN AISLE FOR VISITING SACRED SITES —112

Some people have the travel bug. There are roadmaps for wanderlust galore in aisle eight.

#9. AN AISLE FOR SPIRITUAL HEALING —122

Some people need help with healing. Our metaphysical pharmacy is in aisle nine.

#10. AN AISLE FOR LONGEVITY —130

Some people are ready to extend their life and reverse their thoughts on aging and death itself. Are you one of these? This is the aisle for you.

#11. AN AISLE FOR RELATIONSHIPS —144

Some people need help with relationships. This is a big one. You might get lost in aisle eleven, but we have stocked this aisle with foods that breathe, heal, and clarify.

#12. AN AISLE OF MORE FORGIVENESS —172

Some people may need more work on forgiveness. (That would be most of us.) Deep forgiveness is clarified in aisle twelve.

🛒 #13. AN AISLE FOR SEX —179

Some people need sex more than others. We know this. And it comes in all shapes and sizes these days. You deserve Love. And sex, if you want it. It's all fine in aisle thirteen.

🛒 #14. AN AISLE FOR MONEY & ABUNDANCE —186

All people need this commodity unless you are a sadhu in the High Himalayas. Money is clearly discussed in aisle fourteen.

🛒 #15. AN AISLE FOR HOLY RELATIONSHIPS —194

Some people are ready for sacredness in their life and relationship. A holy relationship is discussed in this aisle.

🛒 #16. AN AISLE FOR DIVINE SERVICE —202

People need to give some of their energy away to keep the abundance flowing to their own spirit pantry. Aisle sixteen helps keep your cornucopia of giving to others fulfilled.

🛒 #17. AN AISLE FOR SOCIAL MEDIA —206

Almost everybody is on Facebook and Twitter these days. Some people need to go on social media. A deeper perspective on social media is here in this aisle.

🛒 #18. AN AISLE FOR LIFE PURPOSE —213

Some people don't know why they are here. We address this most important question in aisle eighteen.

FOREWORD

Sondra Ray and I live together 24 / 7 / 365. We are so melded together in all aspects of our life that it almost seems like we are two halves of the same body. We have our individual strong points, don't get me wrong. I would not expect Sondra to paint a canvas or crunch numbers together on an Excel spreadsheet anymore that she would expect me to maintain our wardrobe (as she loves clothes with a *fashion passion*). But what I am getting at here is that we are totally aligned in our life together; we bring our individual strengths and talents into the vortex of one whirling dervish of a spiritual life together.

During this great sequester of the Covid-19 pandemic our lives have come into communion even more, but in ways that were already moving in that direction. When the shut-down hit we were disappointed, of course, that our road show came to a screeching halt, but that did not affect our dynamics together. We still do everything we did before, just more focused and on purpose, and more implemented through the wonders of the Internet. We travel in the virtual world more than we did before, and we structured our private Liberation Breathing sessions, teaching, and seminars over ZOOM. It was a smooth transition. We were fortunate that the nature of our work relies on relationships, and these were unaffected by the shut-down. In fact, many of our relationships got closer as a result. We became more attentive to our friends, students and to each other. This is a good thing, yes? Well, we saw it that way.

A few weeks into the great sequester (as we are calling it, as it sounds better than "the pandemic") we would notice for the first time in our life that some of the shelves in the supermarket were not being restocked in abundance. It was a bit scary. Where was this heading? We got concerned for people. A lot of people lost their jobs overnight—scarcity seemed to be creeping into our lives as it had never done before. What could we do to turn this situation around with our work and focus? We thought of *The Supermarket for a Meaningful Life.* People needed not only the practical things of external sustenance (that seemed to be showing up as shortages in our local Harris Teeter supermarket), but they also needed the spiritual food of inner sustenance that would keep them out of fear and could help them maintain their interior well-being in this time of crisis.

We took this as a great opportunity with a profound purpose to reboot the way we are relating to each other in our daily lives. We were pressed to see the bigger picture and respond with more compassion, not more fear. We asked ourselves what we needed to do to stay safe and be assured we would still be able to support ourselves and others with our books, Liberation Breathing sessions, and workshops. We were being asked to step up our efforts online in order to go beyond borders and limitations. It has been a really exciting time for us.

The Supermarket for a Meaningful Life became a clear way we could respond. This would be a consolidation of all the spiritual and relationships teachings that we have offered as our version of Divine Service over the years. It would also include inspiration from my Art Looks and books we have read, as well as draw heavily on the relationships we have had over the years with our spiritual masters. In short, together we would compose a "supermarket" where people could come and fill their carts with the *inner food* they need to navigate this great sequester and beyond.

This *Supermarket* has aisles just like a regular store. We included all the essential categories and necessities for a life of fulfillment at all the basic levels. If it works for us, chances are it will work for you. We feed ourselves in this supermarket for deeper meaning. This book is a resource. Sondra and I wrote it together. Some aisles she created, some I created, some we both composed. Like I mentioned above, we are two who have become one. This book is a reflection of that collaborative venture. We hope you will use it as reservoir for replenishment, a supermarket where you can go to refresh yourself and fill your spirit pantry with the nourishment of inspirational food you need.

In her usual vernacular style, Sondra Ray puts deep spiritual truths into everyday language everyone can understand and "get it." I am happy to work and learn with her and get clearer and clearer in the process. You will find as well this simple clarity, the hallmark of her writing, is a great addition to your library of Self enlightenment. You may find yourself going back again and again to *The Supermarket for a Meaningful Life* to fill your basket with the tidbits of wisdom that could transform and nourish you in these times.

This past year has been a great teaching of inner nourishment. "I am sustained by the Love of God" is Lesson #50 in A Course in Miracles. Certainly, we felt the truth of this statement during the past fourteen months of mandatory shifts and challenges. You probably have your own story to tell of how you navigated these times in a totally new way. Now we are in April a year after the shutdown, and many of us have had the vaccine. Others think the whole thing was a great manipulation and conspiracy played out. But we feel the experience was part of what Babaji called the kranti, or global upheaval.

The lessons to learn in this or any upheaval is that ***The Supermarket for a Meaningful Life*** is always open, and our Divine Sustenance is always provided. Our needs are always met in faith and love, not doubt and fear. We look forward to hearing from you. We send you God's blessings.

Washington DC
April 19th, 2021

Markus Ray

INTRODUCTION

We started writing this book at the middle of this COVID-19 pandemic that we are now calling "the great sequester." The supermarket is the main place we go to right now. It is our contact with the outside world. I used to love going to my supermarket. Now we are all a bit hesitant. Wearing masks, witnessing as never before shelves unstocked, people a bit edgy, social distancing, an atmosphere of uncertainty—could be a bit scary.

Markus and I were sitting around home wondering how we could help people better in these uncertain times. Now it has been over a year since the "lockdown." What is it that people need right now?

What could we offer as spiritual teachers that we know works? We envisioned a book like a supermarket composed of aisles, each chapter like an aisle you walk down. You get something different in each aisle.

> 🛒 Some people will need help staying in a state of joy. That is one aisle.
> 🛒 Some people will need help with relationships. That is one aisle.
> 🛒 Some people will need help with healing. That is another aisle.
> 🛒 Some people will need a liberation breathing session. That's another aisle.

🛒 Some people will need enlightened books to read. That is another aisle.

🛒 Some people will need spiritual practices. That is another aisle.

🛒 Some people will need a spiritual master. That is another aisle.

🛒 Some people will need to know about art to lift them out of the doldrums. That is another aisle.

🛒 Some people need processes to stay happy. That is another aisle.

🛒 Some people need to use social media wisely. That is another aisle.

🛒 Some people may need to work on forgiveness. That is another aisle.

🛒 Some people want to know how to handle the fear of death. That is another aisle.

There could be a lot of aisles in *The Supermarket for a Meaningful Life.* Most people want to be liberated—liberated from pain, sickness, fear, guilt, depression, family dysfunctions, and especially death. They want to be liberated from a life that may seem meaningless. This book clearly provides sustenance. It offers the right storehouse for liberation. And most people want to live in a state of happiness. This goes hand and hand with liberation. In the absence of all our problems which is liberation, our deepest desires for pure joy naturally emerge. And we can tap into the energy that helps these desires be *made manifest.* Everyone has a personal manifest destiny, and in *The Supermarket for a Meaningful Life* we are going to help you find it.

We wrote this book because we noticed many people are going through a lot of fear of the future. They are feeling like their lives are on the edge and on hold. What if being on the edge is the new normal? What if pushing through to new paradigms in the middle of "being on hold" is what is needed? Can we handle it? Our Master, Sri Babaji, said in the 1970s, "The Kranti is coming!" We said, "What is the Kranti?" He told us it would be a global revolution. I could not imagine at the time what that would look like.

Another enlightened master told me there are many acts to the Kranti in a *Five Act Play*. We are maybe just in Act One, Scene One right now. Maybe Scene Two is this pandemic. In other words, we don't know what else to expect. And things could get even more unpredictable.

How do we handle being on the edge? For one thing, we have to learn how to maintain our inner peace and joy. That is the antidote for just about everything. We have to stay centered. How do we do that? We have to stay healthy. We have to stay happy so we can stay healthy. We have to stay connected to a sense of our Source—a power greater than ourselves. We have to be a modern-day yogi who is "in the world but not of it." We have to be able to shift gears in a crisis. What do we do when things go totally out of whack? This is a great test.

What if we could make staying on the edge exciting? What if we could see these changes are safe, and for our own good? All new possibilities are on the edge of the NOW. What if this whole thing could be an opportunity to ascend? By ascension we mean go up the ladder of your own spiritual, mental, and physical evolution to higher and broader levels of enlightenment, to greater and greater realizations of perfection. And by enlightenment we mean having a greater sense of purpose, peace, and joy within yourself. "The kingdom of Heaven is within you," the masters say.

We have adapted our world to the circumstances and kept our inner calm. We have switched over to more online seminars, Liberation Breathing sessions, and thrown ourselves totally into our home-based outreach all over the world. We have increased our attention to our spiritual practices which keep us on track and always taking the high road to more joy. We have improved our communications with the people we care about. And we have been fine, living on the edge of uncertainty, knowing that our Divine Creator is taking care of the things we cannot see or manage ourselves. In this way, oddly enough, we are relying on a supernatural certainty we may not have known we had before.

That is why we are writing this book: to make staying on the edge exhilarating; to get more creative; to get more into a state of pure joy; to really exclaim "Carpe Diem!" and seize the day that we have a huge opportunity to ascend, here and now. In this great sequester, and afterwards as well, we have unlimited possibilities to create something beautiful for God. Can we transmute our world into the Kingdom of Heaven that is within us? Shopping in ***The Supermarket for a Meaningful Life*** can help us all do that. We invite you to join us in this storehouse of our Divine Connection together.

Love,

Sondra Ray

#1.

AN AISLE FOR MAINTAINING JOY

I started this book after one month of being in quarantine. This is the time I have to be strong so I can help others and stay healthy and happy. I have been praying a lot and I keep getting that the most important thing of all is that I stay in JOY. For the whole first month I can say I did not feel that—I was way too serious, and I could not allow myself to have any fun or joy at all. It did not seem right to be in joy when the whole world was suffering and into fear. How could I have any fun or joy then? I was doing my spiritual practices and I was really trying to stay on top of things. One of my friends flipped out and quit working with us. That did not help. So, I decided I really, really needed to talk about this subject for myself and everyone. How could we feel abundant joy when there seems to be no money coming in for so many people? One third of Americans could not pay their rent. My heart was bleeding. I felt like crying. I felt so far from joy at times and yet I *knew* joy is the answer.

WHAT IS JOY?

It has been said that joy is the highest expression of God that there is. If we wish for joy in our lives, we must remember that we were made in the image of God and we are God-like. This book will help you to remember who you are and will support you in joyfully loving your God-Self and God more. That's the same as loving joy.

1

When you are feeling great, and everything is working well, and you are getting everything you want, it is easy to feel joy and to love God. But when you don't feel well, and things are not going great, and you are not getting what you want then it seems very difficult to love God and find joy. And that is exactly when you need to love God and create joy, because that is how you get what you want! Inner peace and joy are the great attractors. If you could remember to love God at those times when you are low, then you would be uplifted, heal yourself, and things would start turning around working again.

So how do you turn your mood around? There are a few essential things you must do. First you must decide you are going to shift. It is an action of your own determination to do so. It is an act of will.

There is a great book called *The Untethered Soul* by Michael Singer that has a chapter where you are asked to take a VOW of happiness. If you keep that vow, you do not let anything interfere with your happiness. You are literally not going to be affected by the external situation. I took that vow; but when this COVID-19 crisis started I went off a bit. For the first time in 43 years we had to cancel our India Quest that we always do in the Spring. We had twenty people signed up for it. I was a little bummed about the whole matter. We had to refund a lot of fees and income. Now I want to go back to that vow—because what good am I to anyone if I am in the doldrums? Spiritual teachers have to set an example of how to handle the so-called *tragedies* and turn them into opportunities. So today I think I snapped out of it. I knew I could not continue to be down. I could not continue to avoid the truth: God is pure joy. (I wrote a book about that called *Pure Joy.* You can find it here: bit.ly/PureRay)

Let's face it, most people have not been able to maintain pure joy, even in the good times when there is no world crisis. Because of old frozen ways of thinking, many people are stuck in a worn-out reality that is not working. If we want to be really, really happy, opening to new realities may be required. How could I be in my greatness NOW and make a difference, even in the midst of big change?

I keep thinking of what Einstein once said, "Great spirits have always encountered violent opposition from mediocre minds." Well, I don't mind opposition. I refuse to see you as mediocre. I know there are some things in this book that may stretch your mind, but should I leave them out because of that? I don't think so.

We all need to change now, and we know it. I can be a great spirit and you can be a great spirit. We just have to remember who we truly are in God's eyes. There is no such thing as a mediocre mind when one remembers who one truly is. This is the purpose of this book: to remind us that we are not mediocre. We are made of pure Divine Substance — and we can have an experience of that substance always. This Divine Substance is unaffected by any external crisis that may be thrown our way. We come from this Divine Substance. It is totally possible to know our connection to this Divine Substance and be influenced and protected by it.

Jesus, Babaji, and the Divine Mother are our guides, and they are great spirits who never forget that is who they are. A Course in Miracles would call such beings the *Great Rays*. We call them the *Dream Team*. That is why I feel it is important to use them as an example. They are our inspiration. They came to remind us who we are. The difference is that they do not have any doubt about their Divine Connection, ever. We often forget our Self-Identity, especially in times like these. They are examples of beings who can stay in certainty of their Divine Connection, their Self-identity—all the time. They never fall out of this full awareness of their holiness. Somebody said you become like those you hang out with. I am suggesting you hang out with the spiritual masters who help keep you in the awareness of your true Self, which is one of pure joy.

That is why we need to read uplifting books occasionally to get out of doubt and remember how to feel. This is why we read A Course in Miracles and other enlightened books daily to maintain our joy. We may have to do a purification technique to get back to the joy. *ACIM* offers these miracles, these shifts in our perception that restore our balance and equilibrium. Liberation Breathing®, a simple deep and connected circular energy breathing, helps us to let go of fears and concerns and restore our mind/body as well. The great news is this: doing spiritual purification practices are joyful in themselves and can be real fun. Reading this book could even be blissful. I hope so. It is a joy for me to share this with you.

Pure joy is our natural condition. Some people say that it is our birthright, and this is relatively correct. Yet, seen in its largest perspective, pure joy is that which gives birth to us. Pure joy is the manna of life that keeps us ever flowing, thriving, living.

Here is an important lesson on joy in A Course in Miracles, Lesson #190 in the Workbook. When the *Course* uses the phrase, "the Son of God," it is referring to *you*, regardless of your gender. (See Markus's book on *ACIM* called *The Second Coming: You Are the Christ*; bit.ly/SecondRay)

"I choose the joy of God instead of pain."

What does this mean? It means, first of all, that we can and do choose either joy or pain—all of the time. This is a decision we make, moment to moment. It is up to us. The lesson goes on to explain that it is our thoughts alone that cause us pain. The explanation from Lesson #190 is beautiful:

> *Pain means one is mistaken in his thinking. If one is in pain it is a sign that in his mind illusions are reigning. He is indulging in the ego. The main point is that nothing external can hurt you. Only in your mind. No one but yourself affects you—There is nothing in the world that has the power to dominate you, make you ill, or sad. But it is you who has the power to dominate all things. The world you see does nothing. It merely represents your thoughts and it will change as you change your mind—and choose the joy of God as what you want. When one is in pain, one is denying God. But if you do lay down your thoughts of danger and fear and attack and judgment of yourself, you will begin to find a world without pain. You will begin to find the joy of God. **Pain is illusion. Joy is reality. Pain is deception, joy alone is truth.** And so again we make the only choice that ever can be made; we choose between*

illusions and the truth, or pain and joy, or Hell and Heaven. Let our gratitude to our teacher fill our hearts as we are free to choose our joy instead of pain, our holiness in place of sin, the peace of God instead of conflict, and the light of Heaven for the darkness of the world.

Here are some other beautiful excerpts from *ACIM* about joy:

Living is joy, but death can only weep. *You see in death escape from what you made. But this you do not see; that you made death, and it is but illusion of an end.* ***Death cannot be escape because it is not life in which the problem lies.*** *Life has no opposite, for it is God. (Teacher's Manual p. 50)*

There is one thought in particular that should be remembered throughout the day. ***It is a thought of joy***; *a thought of peace, a thought of limitless release, limitless because all things are freed within it. (Teacher's Manual p. 39)*

When your mood tells you that you have chosen wrongly, and this is so ***whenever you are not joyous***, *then know that this need not be. (Text p. 57)*

God Who encompasses all being, created beings who have everything individually, but who want to share it to increase their JOY. ***Nothing real can be increased except by sharing.*** *That is why God created you. Divine abstraction takes joy in sharing. God has kept your kingdom for you, but He cannot share His joy with you until you know it with your whole mind. (Text p. 64)*

To heal is to make happy. *I have told you to think how many opportunities you have had to gladden yourself, and how many you have refused. This is the same as telling you that you have refused to heal yourself. The light that belongs to you is the light of JOY. Radiance is not associated with sorrow. JOY calls for an integrated willingness to share it.* ***There is no difference between love and joy.*** *Therefore, the only possible whole state is* *the wholly joyous. To heal or to make joyous is therefore the same as to integrate and make one. (Text p. 66)*

*Whatever you accept into your mind has reality for you. I said before that you must learn to think with God. **To think with Him is to think like Him. This engenders joy, not guilt, because it is natural.** Guilt is a sure sign that your thinking is unnatural. (Text p. 69)*

***The Holy Spirit will always guide you truly because your joy is His.** This is His Will for everyone because He speaks for the Kingdom of God, which is joy. Following Him is therefore the easiest thing in the world, and the only thing that is easy. A son of God is happy only when he knows he is with God. (Text p. 126)*

***If God's Will for you is complete peace and joy, unless you experience only this you must be refusing to acknowledge His Will.** When you are not at peace and not in joy; it can only be because you do not believe you are in Him. Yet He is ALL in ALL. (Text p. 133)*

***The Holy Spirit's curriculum is never depressing because it is a curriculum of joy.** Whenever the reaction to learning is depression, it is because the true goal of the curriculum has been lost sight of. (Text p. 141)*

*Every minute and every second give you a chance to save yourself. Do not lose these chances, not because they will not return, but because **delay of joy is needless.** God wills you perfect happiness NOW! (Text p. 163)*

*O my child, if you knew what God wills for you, your joy would be complete!! When you have said, "God's will is mine," you will see such beauty that you will know it is not of you. **Out of your joy, you will create beauty in His name, for your joy could no more be contained than His.** The bleak little world will vanish into nothingness, and your heart will be so filled with joy that it will* leap into Heaven and into the Presence of God. The way is not hard but it is very different. (Text p.185)

Only when you see you are guiltless will you be happy. As long as you believe the Son of God is guilty, you will walk along the carpet, believing it leads to death. And the journey will seem long and cruel and senseless, for so it is. The journey the Son of God has set himself is useless indeed, but **the journey on which the Father sets him is one of release and joy.** You will see as you learn the Son of God is guiltless. When you have accepted the Atonement for yourself, you will realize there is no guilt in God's Son. (Text p. 122)

God's plan for your awakening is as perfect as yours is fallible. You know not what to do, but He Who knows is with you. He would teach you nothing except how to be happy. **Blessed Son of a wholly blessed Father, joy was created for you.** Your calling here is to devote yourself with active willingness, to the denial of guilt in all its forms. The inheritance of the Kingdom is the right of God's Son, given him in his creation. (Text p. 262)

The Holy Spirit teaches thus: There is no hell. Hell is only what the ego has made of the present. The Holy Spirit would undo all of this now. Fear is not of the present, but only the past and future, which do not exist. There is no fear in the present when each instant stands clear and separated from the past without its shadow reaching out into the future. Each instant is a clean, untarnished birth, and the present extends forever. It is so beautiful and so clean and free of guilt that nothing but happiness is there. No darkness is remembered, and **immortality and joy are now!** (Text p. 282)

I asked you earlier, "Would you be hostage to the ego or host to God?" Let this question be asked you by the Holy Spirit every time you make a decision. **For every decision you make does answer this and invites sorrow or joy accordingly.** Every decision you make is for Heaven or hell and brings you the awareness now or what you asked for. (Text p. 286)

7

Swear not to die, you holy Son of God! The Son of Life cannot be killed. He is immortal as His Father. You were not born to die (Text p. 572) Life's function cannot be to die. This will bind your feet and tie your hands and kill your body only if you think that it was made to crucify God's Son. For even though it was a dream of death, you need not let it stand for this for you. Let this be changed. How lovely is the world whose purpose is forgiveness of God's Son! How free from fear, how filled with blessing and with happiness, and **what a joyous thing it is to dwell in such a happy place.** *(Text p. 573)*

Some people who are miserable do not take responsibility for their own suffering. They think, "Life is doing this to me." This is what we would classically call in our work, "victim consciousness." People in this category do not ask, "What is in me that has attracted this sorrow, pain, suffering, etc.?" Only with this question can we look at the thoughts and feelings that attracted the situation, and immediately pivot around to go in the reverse direction toward thoughts and feelings more conducive to pure joy. Many become so weighted down in their unhappiness about their life that they welcome death as a release from all their problems. They do not see their responsibility in making up the thoughts/conditions that are dragging them down. They may see death as an escape from a life in which they see only their problems. Yet, it is important to remember:

Death cannot be escape because it is not life in which the problem lies. (ACIM; Teacher's Manual; p. 50)

How do we begin to heal this sorrow, this pain, this unhappiness *with life*, when it is really our thoughts and feelings "about life" where the culprit of the problem hides? That is what this book is about. When you shop in *The Supermarket for a Meaningful Life* the aisles are stocked with spiritual food you need to bring yourself to pure joy. They are good soul foods of inner repair and restoration. Self-love is on every shelf. Self-care and Self-esteem are the necessary staples for healing yourself of lower levels of being that you do not need anymore. Healing could thus be summed up this way:

To heal is to make happy.
There is no difference between love and joy.
(ACIM; Text; Chapter 5; Intro.)

Some will say that it is mighty hard to heal when you may just have found out you have cancer, or when a parent has just died, or you have lost your job and don't know where your future money is coming from. So, you must start where you are with what you have. In the case of cancer, it is an internal battle between the "life urge and the death urge." (See our book on this subject *Physical Immortality: How to Overcome Death*, bit.ly/ImmortalRay) You must begin to find the things to be happy about and grateful about and focus on them. A healer we met in Japan told us of his client who healed himself of lung cancer, not taking any treatments, just sitting before his altar in his home and saying, "Dear Lungs, I appreciate you so much, you have served me so well in this life." The power of appreciation healed him. He took no medical treatments. Now, we are not advocating not taking medical treatments. We are advocating to include the power of your mind in the healing of any disease—a mind that is well focused on the thoughts and feelings of pure joy and appreciation. This may be even more important than medical solutions.

In the case of a parent dying, Markus's mother died a few years ago. In some ways it felt like a relief actually and a completion. Her quality of life was shrinking and shrinking, and her purpose for being in a physical body was shrinking as well. The transition into the non-physical state was an affirmation of a very long life, well lived. She was 90 years old, with large loss of memory, and with much daily inner struggle. Markus was there for her transition, which was very peaceful. What could have been seen as a tragedy, or a "death," was just felt as a transition out of the physical state, and a re-emergence into the broader and more expansive non-physical, or spiritual state of life. So, in truth, there was no death per se.

In the case of losing one's job, that could be a blessing too. Life is moving you toward something better. When the lockdown occurred and we had to face the fact we would not be able to travel, which is how we made

90% of our income doing seminars and Liberation Breathing sessions in locations around the world, we were a bit shocked at first. But this gave us more impetus to develop our online programs. We just had to see things differently as a new opportunity. We got busy immediately converting our programs into online seminars and online LB sessions that we had already been doing over the years, but not to the degree we were being called to serve in this new way. We had to go into high gear on this conversion, and we did, gladly. Now we are giving online live seminars over ZOOM all over the world.

What we are saying is you can always make an internal shift, no matter what the external situation is presenting to you. You are the master of your own mind, and it is the quality of your mind that affects your levels of happiness. This quality can always be raised by you. "I rule my mind, which I alone must rule." is Lesson #236 in the Workbook of A Course in Miracles. That is SO TRUE! You are the determiner of your destiny.

I would like to say something here about A Course in Miracles for people whose cultures or upbringing may not have been Christian in tone. ACIM is "Christian in tone" for a couple of good reasons. There has been so much false religious theology over the centuries meted out by the church that Christianity needed to be corrected. Jesus does this in A Course in Miracles. It is not a religion at all. It is not another belief system used to divide and separate us as a human race into irreconcilable religious sects and parties. It is an action of unification and reconciliation. It is a sound set of spiritual and practical principles to live by. It is a pathway to unconditional love which as members of a whole human race we all need right now. It is consistent with all the great holy masters' teachings all over the world through time immemorial. It is a course that leads us through ascension toward our true and holy Self.

In India, the highest scholars and sages do not even refer to Hinduism as a religion. They refer to *sanatana dharma* as the root of all religions. It is a set of Divine Principles to live by. All people interested in melding their individual self with their universal self are commonly called sadhus or yogis. But in these modern times we all can do that, no matter what walk of life. We may find ourselves in a corporate setting and still wish to make our whole life "One with the Universal Intelligence of creation"—or, one with God. Dr. Helen Schucman, scribe of A Course in Miracles, led a spiritual life in scribing this great scripture, and also kept her job as a clinical psychologist at Columbia University Medical School. One can be *in the world but not of it.* And in the world is where the light of our spirituality is absolutely needed.

In summary, A Course in Miracles is for anyone, in any culture, of any religious background, in any profession, station in life, who yearns to make contact with Divine Peace and Joy within themselves. This is everyone's birthright to have. Practicing ACIM is more akin to a sanatana dharma—a way of life, a set of lofty and holy principles to live by—than it is to a religion, even though it is Christian in tone. One could be Hindu, Buddhist, Muslim, Jain, Zoroastrian, Shinto, or even Atheist and get some kernel of wisdom from A Course in Miracles. Tara Singh, Markus's Teacher of ACIM for 17 years, and who was trained by its scribe, Dr. Helen Schucman herself, called it "a gift for all mankind."

Markus Writes: Getting back to pure joy and the necessity of it

There is a saying, "Beauty is in the eyes of the beholder." Beauty is an internal matter, depending on preference and taste of the individual. We would say, "Joy is in the heart of the beholder" as well. It is an internal matter. But more than a mere assessment of the external conditions that you may or may not like, pure joy is a vibration of appreciation for Life itself. Are you glad to be alive, moment to moment? Do you appreciate one breath? Do you wonder about the miracle of your heart beating? Can you have gratitude for all that is available to you now? Pure joy begins with a deep gratitude for Life itself, and then everything in it is a great spirit as Einstein said, including first and foremost yourself. And you transcend all mediocrity by being this Self.

Along with gratitude comes a deep yearning to share it. Pure joy is contagious! You can hardly contain it, nor should you:

Nothing real can be increased except by sharing. That is why God created you. (ACIM; Text; Chapter 4; Sec. VII; ¶5)

This confirms a principle that is universal: *whatever you put out you receive back.* If you share pure joy, you will receive it back in confirmation from others, from your surroundings, from your colleagues, from your environment, from every aspect of your life. Should you choose to extend anger, pain, suffering and sorrow, and even death, you will receive more of that back to you. It is a decision on your part what you want to share. "What am I sharing in my life now?" you might ask yourself.

But what if we find ourselves in pain? Adding more guilt onto that fact will not help. We have had a momentum going that has resulted in pain that we have to stop. So, the first step is to forgive ourselves for whatever that momentum has been. You can say, "The thought I had that produced this pain is _____." Listen to what your subconscious mind is telling you. Then you have to turn that thought around. Changing your mind is the first and foremost action you can take to free yourself from pain. Choosing joy is our responsibility. At first this is reparative. Then when you replace the negative thoughts manifesting pain for the positive thoughts that are their antidotes, you can also begin having feelings of pure joy resulting from this shift.

Perhaps we focused too much on the negative aspects of things? Perhaps we judged ourselves as unworthy or not good enough? Perhaps we had deep-seated judgments about situations and people? Perhaps we had catastrophic thinking with a lot of fear of the future? Perhaps we used anger and attack to manipulate and get what we wanted, leaving a trail of casualties in our wake? These are the very stubborn and persistent thought forms and memories we need to forgive.

Forgiveness is the key to happiness.
(ACIM; Workbook; Lesson #121)

Forgiveness is selective remembering. All the happy thoughts and memories are true, and all the painful and traumatic ones are simply there to be released. This is a spiritual discipline in itself. This is the forgiveness offered in A Course in Miracles. It is the doorway to our own personal nirvana, and the nirvana of the world. Would we rather have pure joy or the strife and struggles we find ourselves and the world in right now? To shop in *The Supermarket of a Meaningful Life* in the Aisle of Pure Joy, the cart into which we throw our goods and services is the cart of true and unequivocal forgiveness. Truly, it is the cart of our Divine Purpose—pure joy.

> *Forgive us our illusions, Father, and help us to accept our true relationship with You, in which there are no illusions, and where none can ever enter. Our holiness is Yours. What can there be in us that needs forgiveness when Yours is perfect? The sleep of forgetfulness is only the unwillingness to remember Your forgiveness and Your Love. Let us not wander into temptation, for the temptation of the Son of God is not Your will. And let us receive only what You have given, and accept but this into the minds which You created and which you Love. Amen. (ACIM; Text; Chapter 16; Sec. VII; ¶12)*

Let us receive pure joy into our minds. Everything but that is a limitation placed upon the ascension of the human spirit. Everything but that is a limitation we place upon ourselves.

 **#2.**

AN AISLE FOR ENLIGHTENMENT

In all our books we have defined enlightenment as having CERTAIN KNOWLEDGE that your thoughts produce your results and taking responsibility for raising the quality of your thoughts. Simply put, we say, "thought is creative." You are the creator of your reality with your thoughts. This is a universal law of attraction and metaphysics. Feelings are spearheaded by thoughts. Thoughts and feelings form an internal frequency in your being, and this frequency attracts situations, people, and things who share this frequency. So, in order to mold a more perfect *reality*, we have to first mold the quality and contents of our thoughts. We have to raise the frequency of how we feel and think into a new paradigm. Here is what ACIM says about that:

> *You may believe that you are responsible for what you do, but not for what you think. The truth is that you are responsible for what you think because it is only at this level that you can exercise choice. What you do comes from what you think. (ACIM; Text; p. 25)*

> *It is impossible that the Son of God be merely driven by events outside of Him. It is impossible that happenings that came to Him were not His choice. His power of decision is the determining factor of every situation in which he seems to find Himself, by choice or accident. (ACIM; Text; p. 418)*

The *Course* is always asking why you condone insane thinking. In the next moment you can experience Heaven or hell, depending on which thought you choose to think. You always have free choice to go toward the spirit (positive thinking) or the ego (negative thinking). Bliss is only one thought away; and that thought is up to you.

If you return all your thinking to the Holy Spirit, you will be in joy. The Holy Spirit is merely that concentration of all spiritual energy that permeates higher levels of consciousness (obviously imbued in all the spiritual masters who have come to help humanity). This thinking results in our evolution toward Divine Love, Peace and Joy.

Say only this:

> *I am responsible for what I see.*
> *I choose the feelings I experience, and*
> *I decide upon the goal I would achieve.*
> *And everything that seems to happen to me*
> *I ask for and receive as I have asked.*
> *(ACIM; Text; p. 418)*

You must deceive yourself no longer that you are helpless in the face of what is done to you.

What are the highest thoughts you can think? It is a spiritual discipline to constantly observe your thoughts and raise the quality of your thoughts. The minute you spot a negative thought, let it go and change it to the opposite as an affirmation. You also have to observe how you are feeling. Are you moving up the ladder to pure joy?

At any given time, you have a choice. Are you going to be under the ego's thought system or the Holy Spirit's thought system? Much of the time we are not even aware that we are using the ego's memories of the past to replay similar situations in the present. We have made this Mind Map to show you the difference between the results of the ego vs. the Holy Spirit:

MIND MAP

MORTAL MIND— EGO'S Thought System	IMMORTAL MIND— HOLY SPIRIT'S Thought System
Separation	Oneness
Guilt	Innocence
Fear	Love
Pain	Well-Being
Anger	Harmony
Conflict	Peace
Worry	Certainty
Misery	Gratitude
Depression	Happiness
Sickness	Health
Scarcity	Abundance
DEATH	MORE LIFE
I AM NOT!	I AM THAT I AM!

You are *enlightened* when you replace the ego's thought system with the Holy Spirit's thought system. Is your relationship placed under the Holy Spirit's thought system? If it is in the ego's thought system, it will be contracted into a limited state of self-enclosure. The guiding thought will be, "What can I gain from the other person?" Your "case" (negative patterns) will be reinforced. There will be clinging, fear, and dependency. There will be conflict, uncertainty, fear, and an endless chain of struggles. You may fight a lot and think that is just *normal*. The body could be seen as a sex object, perhaps. Pleasure will be sought to avoid pain, but the two may be somewhat indistinguishable.

Under the Holy Spirit's thought system, your relationship will expand into greater realities. The guiding thought will be, "What can I give to my mate?" Your case will be purified. (What I mean by your "case" is the conglomerate of your tendencies, your family patterns, your limiting beliefs, your traumas from the past, your debilitating beliefs, etc.) There will be trust and the freedom to *be*—with reinforcement of Self expansion. The body will be seen as the temple of God. It will be used as a *communication device* to express your pure joy.

There is one thought alone that can ruin your life. Please fill in the blank to find out what it is for you. My most negative thought about myself is _____. Until you heal that thought in your mind, life is going to be less than pure joy for you. We call this thought your personal lie. Common *personal lies* are thoughts like: "I am not good enough;" "I am wrong;" "I am not wanted;" "I am alone;" "I am bad;" "I am guilty;" "I am not perfect;" "I do not want to be here;" "I am a failure," etc. It is not the real truth about you because God did not create you with that thought. But you believe it is true somewhere in the core of your subconscious, and usually you have been thinking it for several lifetimes—so it is an addiction.

You may have picked up this thought at birth as a *preverbal thought*, or you may have gotten it before that. The problem is you have been trying to prove it is right. This is how your ego has you tricked. Remember this: *Whatever you believe to be true, you create.* So, believing that thought, you are going to create experiences that make it seem true. For example, if your thought is, "I am bad," you will constantly create situations that make you look and feel bad. You might just do bad things if you are acting it out. If you are projecting it, everyone else will seem bad. If you are suppressing it and overcompensating, you will try to be really, really good—but it will be a fake. For further understanding of this please read our book *Liberation: Freedom from Your Biggest Block to Pure Joy*. You can order it here: (bit.ly/LibRay). We have listed over 360 different *personal lies* we have recorded from people over the past 12 years.

You may say, "My life is going great! I have two cars in the garage, a great career, a home in town, a home at the beach, and a million bucks in the bank. I don't have a personal lie." Unless your parents were both immortal yogis, most likely you still have some vestige of negative programming that could be released and thus allow your life to flower even more in the direction of universal pure joy. Some people who are hugely successful may have a personal lie, "I am not important," "I don't matter," or "I am a failure." They are huge over-compensators, so they are able to take that negative thought and use it as a catalyst to go in the opposite direction, achieving unprecedented feats of material success. But underlying all their material success, there still may be a nagging quality in their feeling body that their achievements are "not enough," their souls are remaining somewhat unsettled. They are not really fulfilled or truly satisfied.

You may have resistance to give up your personal lie completely because your whole life has been about proving it, overcompensating for it, wrestling with it, and working around it. When it goes, there will be a death of that part of your mind and your whole reality will change. Some people are so afraid of change that they would rather hang on to what is not working because it is familiar. Over-compensators don't want to face the fact their "driven nature" affords them no real peace of mind. So, it would be unfamiliar to NOT have that thought about yourself, and people are often afraid of the unfamiliar. We can assure you that without that thought, things will be so much better. In fact, it will be Heaven without that thought.

The problem is this: just changing the personal lie to its opposite is not enough. It is stuck in the cells, so it also has to be breathed out in many Liberation Breathing / breathwork sessions, or through other spiritual practices in which this release is addressed. Something in you knows also that if you gave up that thought, you would have a tremendous increase in energy. If you are afraid of more energy, it is probably because you are afraid of God. God is simply the Energy of the Universal Life Force.

It took all of us breathworkers a long time to work out our personal lies. So, don't get discouraged if it takes a while for you. Do not take this discussion lightly. It is a key for sure. You cannot be enlightened and keep your personal lie. Furthermore, you need to know your mate's personal lie. Yours could be dovetailing with theirs. Working out your personal lies together is imperative on the path to enlightenment as a couple.

The hugging saint, Amritanandamayi, or commonly called Amma, has pointed out in the movement toward enlightenment there are three various "shadows" of our past that we need to clear in our process of Self-realization. One is the "family shadow." This is composed of all the limiting beliefs and dynamics that we inherited from our parents, family, and ancestors. The next is the "religious shadow." This is all the conflicts we may have with the notion of God, the possible false religious theology we inherited from our childhood religious dogmas and beliefs. Thirdly is the "personal shadow." This is a conglomerate of our negative personality traits and beliefs that we have about ourselves. In short, this third shadow amounts to our personal lie.

The Eastern spiritualist Sai Baba said that "The sole purpose of your incarnation is the crucifixion of the ego." Another modern-day enlightened soul, Ram Dass, shared this idea on the subject of enlightenment:

> *Why are you here? You are here to take the curriculum. You can use your own "case" (your negativity, your karma etc.) as a stepping stone.*

Our Indian teachers say the purpose of life is to recognize the Supreme. A Course in Miracles would agree with that, plus it would say another purpose is to experience constant joy. Of course, we are also here to learn and to clear our karma. The dissolution of the ego is a step-by-step process of giving up separation and limitation which can lead us to the experience of ourselves as Divine Masters. Ultimately though, the real purpose of life is to experience and emanate pure joy that uplifts us and all those around us. We are here to be love and extend love, and that is a state of pure joy.

Let us say one thing about karma though. It does not have to be a "heavy thing" if you forgive yourself and take action to resolve and work it out. Karma is simply the principle of true cause and effect. Thoughts and actions you had in the past will replay in the present if you don't take responsibility for them. When you change your thoughts of guilt for ones of pure joy and innocence, you will get different effects. When you forgive yourself and all others for the mistakes manifested in the past, their effects are rendered inconsequential. Freedom from karma is merely paying off all your past debts. So, coming to a still mind in which your entire past is forgiven and released is a very important action in this movement toward enlightenment.

When they asked the Buddha, "How do you solve a problem," He said, "I never get into one." In other words, he had cleared his past, his thought, his personal lie, and arrived at the emptiness of a still mind that had no judgments about anything. He was filled with the Light of Truth, so to speak, in which there was only pure joy and nothing else. This is the boon of cleaning the mind of all negativity. What is left in the space of a still mind is the awareness of the Source of Infinite Love and Wisdom.

It should be our overriding desire to discover this Source of Infinite Love and Wisdom, and to express this in daily life. The purpose of relationships is to enhance these goals.

Example of High Thoughts for Night-Time Programming

There is a set of great books called *The Life and Teachings of the Masters of the Far East* by Baird Spalding. Now, whether you believe them to be "fact or fiction" does not really matter. Just like whether you believe our Master Sri Herakhan Babaji manifested His body out of the Light without coming through the womb of a woman does not really detract one bit from the huge contribution to the evolution of humanity He came to impart. That mission is still realized by His presence upon the planet, just as these works by Baird Spalding have served for a century now in the awakening of humanity toward higher levels of enlightenment.

I now realize that there is within me a spiritual joy-body ever young, ever beautiful. I have a beautiful spiritual mind, eyes, nose, mouth, skin—the body of the Divine Infant, which now, tonight is perfect. Well, dear _____(place your name), there is a divine alchemist within. The divine alchemist is within my temple, constantly coining new and beautiful baby cells. The spirit of youth is within my temple—this human form divine, and all is well. Om Shanti, Shanti, Shanti (peace, peace, peace). I think a happy thought for all the world. May all the world be happy and blessed. Within me there is a perfect form—the form Divine. I am now all that I desire to be! I visualize daily my beautiful being until I breathe it into expression. I am a Divine Child; all my needs are being now and forever supplied! Infinite Love fills my mind and thrills my body with the perfect life. (From: *The Life and Teachings of the Masters of the Far East.* Volume 1; by Baird T. Spalding)

Much of anything we value in life, such as our spiritual awakening into our greatest and happiest Self-identity, requires a coming together of our intentions, our focus, our attentions, and the infinite powers of Divine Grace. We need a willingness to correct. In fact, Tara Singh called this attitude an actual "love for correction." It could be more akin to undoing mistakes. When the world was stuck in the belief the earth was flat with an edge over which ships could fall into a great abyss, and that sailing too far out into the great seas of the Unknown could only bring demise and ruin, a few men knew differently. They went for a new paradigm. And now, five hundred years later, it's almost impossible to believe we could have been so stupid. The planet is an orb around which we safely travel.

Few have caught up with the true power of the mind in the service of Divine Love of Truth. One could list on only a few pages the likes of a Jesus, or a Buddha, or a Mother Teresa. Quan Yin is only one. Lord Krishna came at a time when the world needed the sanatana dharma—and He was the one to make it clear. In the midst of tribal factions and various superstitious beliefs that caused struggle and strife among the desert peoples, Muhammed came to unify and codify people into a brotherhood of Divine Love. Various Indian sages, male and female, over the centuries have brought the light of truth to humanity. The sage of Arunanchala, Sri Ramana Maharshi, gave us the simple question, "Who am I?" to undo all lower orders of being in our ascent toward our true and holy Self. Enlightenment has been a deep yearning of humanity. It is no less now than it has ever been. And we are no less guided by the great spirits who have laid the path for us to walk, if you could even say there is a path.

Life is the only path. Pure joy is the only destination. The 20th century sage, Mr. J. Krishnamurti, said, "Truth is a pathless land." He warned us against any preconceived dogma or path toward enlightenment. The crucible of transformation within us is already lit. Will we keep it burning is the only question? Will we continue to challenge ourselves to let go of limiting beliefs, concepts, memories that keep us from pure joy? Pure joy is offered in the freedom of the now beyond the known. Will we step into it? Or will we succumb to fear and falseness of beliefs?

We are all in that Aisle of Enlightenment here in the COVID-19 great sequester. What do we have to give to others and ourselves during and after this revolution of our souls? Will we discover our True Self and live up to our highest aspirations, to our brothers and sisters, to our humanity? Or will we return to the same old patterns of competition and feelings of lack in the complicated dramas of business as usual? The decision is ours.

 # #3.

AN AISLE FOR ENCOURAGEMENT AND GRATITUDE

There is nothing new about the qualities of encouragement and gratitude, but there may be a new way to use them in an enlightened relationship. Imagine this:

> Early in the relationship, you decide to tell your mate about the issues you are working on at this time in your life. You ask your mate for his or her support and encouragement with this problem. You also promise to work on your problem(s) with diligence. You are grateful for your mate's support. You do not feel threatened. You express this gratitude when you are getting encouragement and support. You also give your mate permission to point out to you unconscious backsliding on your part; furthermore, you are grateful to be awakened about this unconsciousness. Your mate always tries to be encouraging rather than critical by holding the thought in his mind that this block can be healed.

Sound impossible? Well, it isn't. You know you need feedback, and you are not defensive about it. If you can analyze yourself fearlessly, you can stand the critical analysis of others. You need to have a *love of correction*. If you get defensive it won't work. Besides, defenses attract attack. If you don't recognize your hang-ups, you are absolutely okay if your mate talks about them to you. You want to know how you are coming across and you are grateful for all feedback. You and your mate serve each other like an open book. There are no secrets and there are no shortcomings that are insurmountable. All mistakes can be corrected in a spirit of joy and innocence. Evolutionary steps in your soul's development are welcomed. You become each other's *ascension buddy.*

The old way of handling each other's hang-ups has been called co-dependent bargaining. A couple had an unconscious agreement that went something like this:

"I won't confront your heavy smoking habit if you don't make me confront my rampant spending habits." There was mutual denial—no attempt on either side to encourage soul progress. In the new paradigm there is no room for these co-dependent maneuvers because they only leave you more stuck. The opposite of denial would be overkill or dwelling too much on your mate's faults. There should be an appropriate balance. Self-examination is the key. Remember this quote from Yogananda:

> **Those who dwell on the faults of others are like human vultures.** (Yogananda)

That is why we recommend examining and questioning yourself and asking for support in the process. Practice encouragement of each other.

Consider this: How about having the most gratitude for that which upsets you? If it upsets you, that means it is one of your shadows. You want them healed. The fact that it is coming up means that it is going out. Why not be gentle on each other and not judgmental? If your mate had an illness, would you judge them about it, or help them heal it? The same patience is needed to heal all tendencies in the body and mind. Momentum is a force to contend with. Bad habits or addictions may not be so easy to overcome. We have to offer our mate our patience. And also our support and clarity at the same time.

The Power of Gratitude

One of the most powerful transformative mindsets is the mindset of gratitude. There is a way of walking in gratitude all the time. It is the most loving attitude we can nurture. And since we may have fallen into more critical modes of thinking in which we seek and point out the shortcomings of any situation or even people we are close to, we have to do some work here to turn this tendency around. One of the greatest exercises Markus and I have practiced over the years is to keep a gratitude journal. It is very simple.

First, buy yourself a nice blank journal with a nice cover. You can use one that already inspires you. Markus and I have collected a lot of blank journals from all over the world. One of our favorites has been a handmade journal with a tooled leather cover from Estonia we picked up in Tallinn. The paper is nice too. It is handmade and has decorative dividers of brocade sheets every 25 pages or so.

There are two parts to this writing process. Open the book to the first page and title it: My Gratitude Journal. This identifies the things and sets your clear intention. On the first pages with a left page and a right page, start writing your gratitude like this:

On the left page write ten things today you are grateful for, beginning with the statement "I am so happy and grateful for _____." You describe in good detail one thing you are very grateful for. It could be large or small. It could be common or uncommon.

Some examples:

1) I am so happy and grateful for our Washington apartment.
2) I am so happy and grateful for our nice view of the street.
3) I am so happy and grateful for running water.
4) I am so very grateful for our blue glass bottles from Spain.

The important thing as you write them down is to feel the love you have for these things. Feel how your life would be not as easy, or beautiful, or happy without them. Yes, you could make it, but with the blessings of Divine Providence for these things you live a sacred and holy life, easier than many, and absolutely cherished in the care of your Creator. This is what you write on the left page. You list ten things or qualities for which you are very grateful that you have.

On the right side of the book, you do something a bit differently in your gratitude expressions. You still list ten things, as you did on the left. But on the right page these are things, situations, relationships, or desires that you have not manifested yet. But you do acknowledge that you are still grateful for these things. You write them down as if you already have manifested them. "I am so happy and grateful I now have_____." Some examples:

1. I am so happy and grateful I now have a publisher in India.
2. I am so happy and grateful Markus's last painting has sold to a prominent collector.
3. I am so happy and grateful *The Supermarket for a Meaningful Life* is in the hands of millions of people.
4. I am so happy and grateful our international Quests to sacred sites are back up and running, and they are thriving.

Some people would call this "pie in the sky" thinking, or "fake it 'til you make it" fantasy. In actuality, all statements (thoughts) create a vibrational frequency (feeling) in our fields of being, and it is this vibrational frequency that affects our forward movements. High thoughts keep our ship of life buoyant, with full sails, and flowing forward. Lower and negative thoughts shrink our aura and take the wind out of our sails. Which would you rather have—a ship with sails billowing out on the course to fulfillment and pure joy or the drooping sails in the doldrums of negative thoughts and feelings, limited by the lack of faith and trust?

Keep this gratitude journal as inspired. Try not to make it a ritual that you force yourself to do. It has to be an inspiration of joy. Do it once a week if every day becomes too imposed as another thing to do.

Does a thought have to be thought with certainty before it can manifest? Columbus did not know there was an America before he landed on it. But he had an inner hunch that something was there. The Wright brothers did not have the experience of flight before they invented the first successful airplane, which they flew at Kitty Hawk. Einstein had not yet discovered the Theory of Relativity before he trusted that he was a great spirit connected to the Infinite Intelligence of Creation. Jesus had not proved to Himself the possibility of resurrection until he raised Lazarus from the dead! Mother Teresa did not know she could render decades of service to the poorest of the poor until she picked up the first dying person from the streets of the slums in Calcutta. All great actions that plummet humanity forward began with an inkling, then with a trust, then with a thought "as if it already is," then with an action, and then a manifestation. And vibrationally, all these various stages are in harmony with the laws of the universe. They emanate from a place of gratitude, of well-being, of implicit trust in oneself, which together tap into the unlimited power of pure joy!

We are children of the miraculous. Who could fathom the workings of a hand? Of a set of lungs? Of a plane that can take us around the world in a day. Of an internet of things that keeps us connected to everyone simultaneously? What will we dream up next in the times after this COVID-19? Will it be more fear? More distrust? Or is this the wakeup call we needed to see the wholeness of life? The wholeness of the human race? We are our brother's keeper. Why is that so? Because our brother is us. What we do to him we do to ourselves. Gratitude and acknowledgment, and yes, encouragement are the only proper attitudes toward our closest mate and family, and to our colleagues and strangers alike. All together we form the Son-ship and Daughter-ship in this family of humanity. Can we give our love, our encouragement, and our gratitude for a holy relationship that is free of all shadows of doubt, discouragement, and despair? This aisle offers it.

Love is the way I walk in gratitude.
(ACIM; Workbook; Lesson # 195)

#4.

AN AISLE FOR SPIRITUAL PRACTICES

In the first fifty principles of miracles in A Course in Miracles there are some very profound statements. Basically, they are showing us how to shift our mind and be a "miracle worker." In fact, miracles are natural expressions of our spiritual self in these dimensions of the mind/body, or mental and physical world.

One of the statements that is important to note is principle #7:

> ***Miracles are everyone's right, but purification is necessary first.***
> *(ACIM; TEXT; Chapter 1; Section I; ¶7)*

In the East there is such a thing as a "sadhana." Roughly translated this is a set of spiritual practices that one does on a daily basis for the purpose of Self-realization, or for spiritual purification in this case. This set of spiritual practices is deemed essential to life. The practices do not have to be complicated or demanding like a set of imposed penances. But they do have to be regular practices that one does to step out of the tendencies of the undisciplined and unexamined life into a life more focused on our divine nature and spiritual connection to our Source.

This Aisle #4 is for people who are thirsty for something to do to formulate a spiritual practice—a kind of modern-day, Western sadhana that satisfies the purification that enables us to work miracles. Jesus of A Course in Miracles calls miracles our *right*. And He means what He says. And He is also clear that purification is necessary first in order for us to work them.

Liberation Breathing®

I love to talk about this subject because it totally healed me. It is a spiritual gift. It is one of the main purification tools we use to produce pure joy. What it does is help you release the blocks you have that keep you from experiencing your natural state, which *is* pure joy. This happens through the power of using your own breath—it is connecting the inhale with the exhale (with no pause or holding at the top of the inhale or at the bottom of the exhale) in a relaxed smooth rhythm. It is not a hard discipline. It is an inspiration. It cleanses your mind and body in a very dynamic way with Divine Energy. Leonard Orr and I developed this in the early 1970s in San Francisco at the Theta House.

We called it "rebirthing" back then. Leonard and I wrote the first book on it, *Rebirthing in the New Age*. I wrote most of that book with an emphasis on Leonard's discoveries. It spread around the world like wildfire. Now, rebirthing is practiced everywhere around the world by the generic name of breathwork. It has overcome some bad press in which other healing modalities resulting in deaths, such as attachment therapy and ill-practiced sweat lodges, were erroneously dubbed rebirthing by the press. They were *not at all* rebirthing. Absolutely not. It took some years for breathwork to overcome this unfortunate, mistaken, and ill-informed press. This is another reason we call the process Liberation Breathing® now. Leonard Orr passed in 2019, but I am still alive and strong placing the process under the guidance and blessings of the Divine Mother. The breath, in fact, is our most powerful body/mind/spirit connector that joins us with the Divine Mother (the Universal Life Force that flows in every atom of Creation).

Conscious connected breathing, Liberation Breathing, is one of the fastest ways to integrate all levels of our being. My master, Babaji, called it the new kriya yoga. It is a breathing meditation anyone can do, best in the presence of a practitioner who has already been through the clearing process on themselves. Liberation Breathing clears our subconscious thoughts all the way back to conception in this life, and even before. It is the ultimate spiritual purification in my book.

This breathing is not therapy (although it does clear up latent psychological issues). It is a spiritual purification technique. It acquaints you with a dimension of spiritual energy which you may never have experienced. It can be an ultimate healing experience because breath, together with raising the quality of our thoughts, can produce miracles.

As I said, in the 1970s we used to call it rebirthing and we used to try to remember and re-experience our birth in order to release any memories that remained from the original birth trauma. Everyone has some. That was a remarkable aspect of the work. But then we found out it does so much more than that! We found out it can really transform your subconscious. It created a safe environment for symptoms of the past to come out—we found we could get free of all negativity.

One can learn the Liberation Breathing breath technique in five minutes, but it will take a lifetime to master it, as this form of breathwork also deals with unraveling your mind. It is so simple, and yet, people resist letting go and forgiving old patterns and grievances from the past. The breath helps release these cellular memories, but usually, depending how stubborn and clinging you are to these old thoughts, that can take some time working with a trained Liberation Breathing practitioner.

Think of breathing in divine energy and pure joy coming up from the base of your spine through the root chakra. As you continue the inhale pull the energy up through the other chakras to the upper chest, through the lung area and as high as the throat chakra, and then even further up to the crown chakra. As you begin the exhale visualize the breath flowing out of the crown chakra and just falling by the weight of gravity itself, without any effort, without any pushing, back down to the base of the spine at the root chakra again. We like to say, "pull up on the inhale and relax on the exhale, like letting go completely."

This way the breath is a smooth, connected, circular breathing. Please note that breathing in this way will give you more energy than you are used to in your body, and it can be a little scary to do this by yourself if you have never done it. So, we do not recommend you try it alone, without the guidance of a qualified breathworker. The safety is part of the mix that a practitioner provides. Also, they have been through the process themselves and they can support you through yours. We recommend a series of ten Liberation Breathing sessions with the same breathworker to begin. Then ten sessions with the opposite sex to get the mother/father polarity clear. Then you could try the process by yourself, and probably be just fine. Markus and I give our sessions together, so both polarities are covered in our first ten sessions. You can book LB sessions with us here: https://bit.ly/LBSession.

Another reason to have a practitioner is he or she will question you about your thoughts and the things you would like to release or overcome in your life. You could too easily not face these things if you just "breathe on your own." Therefore, you don't put all your thoughts on the table to clear them. A breathworker helps you do this. With these thoughts recognized you are more likely to have their release. It is like Jesus said, "Where two or more are gathered in my Name, my Presence is there." So, the clarity of a holy relationship is invoked by the two— breathworker and breather. This is very essential in the beginning to get the most out of the Liberation Breathing process. This is why we do not recommend you do it alone at first. You can't to have the full benefits. The relationship aspect of the process is absolutely necessary.

When Markus and I came together for our mission, our masters told us to add the Divine Mother energy to the sessions and we were guided to call it Liberation Breathing and have that name legally registered. The Divine Mother WILL liberate you. We were told by adding prayers and mantras of the Divine Mother at the end of the session, it was nine times more powerful. We have witnessed this space of the miraculous present in the sessions we conduct. The clients notice this presence of the sacred is invoked and actually felt in the sessions with us.

Liberation Breathing increases your ability to receive love. It definitely improves relationships, especially if both you and your partner are having sessions. This adds tremendous joy to your relationship. The ideal for me is when you and your partner both learn how to give sessions. Then you can give sessions also to each other. That really makes a difference in a relationship. It brings more spiritual intimacy into your relationship. (We can train you how to do this. See our book: *Spiritual Intimacy: What You Really Want with a Mate*; (https://bit.ly/IntimacyRay.)

Liberation Breathing can help you become more creative and intuitive. This happens as you clear your ego so you can experience the availability of Infinite Intelligence. You have direct access to this, but it takes some silencing of your own thoughts to make contact with it. LB helps you achieve this quieting of the mind as well.

Liberation Breathing is truly a rejuvenation process. Your body is rejuvenated with Divine Energy. I had the privilege of taking this breathwork to Russia and training breathworkers over there. It was a tough assignment, let me tell you. (The Iron Curtain was still up, and the KGB was following me.) Anyway, the breathworkers I trained in Russia did sessions on doctors and the doctors wired each other up during the sessions, and they did prove in that study that rejuvenation of the body/cells occurs while practicing deep, connected, circular breathing over an extended period of time.

Liberation Breathing is sacred. To me, it is a way you can experience making love with God because you are actually communing with the Holy Spirit. Many people tell us they got more out of three sessions of Liberation Breathing than they did in 10 years of conventional therapy. We hear that all the time. Many say it was the greatest experience they had since they were born. We constantly hear comments like this one: "Every growth experience I have had promised more than it delivered except Liberation Breathing. That delivered a whole lot more than it promised."

For further study I refer you to our book *Liberation Breathing: The Divine Mother's Gift.* (https://bit.ly/LiberationRay). We consider this a life-long spiritual practice. Once you get past the original 10 sessions recommended, you will see so much change in yourself that you will want to keep going on and on.

Here is a list of just what Liberation Breathing is:

❖ Rejuvenating your body with Divine Energy
❖ A scientific / spiritual experience
❖ Baptism of the Holy Spirit with power
❖ Inflow of Divine Energy (call it pure Life Force)
❖ Re-learning to breathe
❖ A physical experience of Infinite Being
❖ A growth experience focused on releasing trauma rather than re-experiencing it
❖ An energy-release
❖ A cure for sub-ventilation
❖ Learning to relax at the cosmic level
❖ Cleansing the mind and body of negative mental mass
❖ A technique of spiritual healing
❖ Rebuilding the body with prenatal life energy
❖ Renewal of Divine nature in human form
❖ Regeneration of human perfection
❖ Dynamic energy infusion
❖ Divine orgasm
❖ Release from mortal bondage
❖ Becoming aware of the energy the body has always channeled
❖ The practical mystical experience
❖ Pumping negative thoughts, feelings, and illness out of the body with the breath
❖ A breathing mantra
❖ A breathing meditation
❖ A going beyond all limiting beliefs
❖ A way to feel really good!

Why is this spiritual purification technique so important right now? Mainly, I would say it is the answer to release one's fear. So many people have so much fear right now in these times of the great sequester. We help clients to inhale love and exhale fear. For me, I have several times during this pandemic had to do this type of breathing for three straight hours. I felt so fortunate to be able to do it myself. One can learn it after having a series of sessions with a well-trained breathworker. We are available to give sessions at any time night or day. We also have others trained in various countries.

Ricardo's First Liberation Breathing Experience

I experienced the most important episode of my life in my Liberation Breathing private session with Sondra and Markus Ray. I went to this session without great expectations, only with the desire to go deeper in my experiences and learn more about how people who are advanced in this practice are working with Liberation Breathing. At the beginning of the session, they asked me many questions about my birth, relationship with parents and childhood. They asked me if there was something specific that I would like to work on in that session. I said that I had been practicing rebirthing breathwork for a few months, and that my experiences were pretty tranquil, lineal and repetitive. I sincerely wanted to understand why this was happening. Was it because I did not really have any deep inner issues to be worked out? Or, was it because I had strong blocks that I was not ready to release? They asked me to start breathing and we would find out. At this point I had already reported that I was born from a very long cesarean birth. My mother was hospitalized on Saturday and I was born on Monday. My family was very worried about the delay and also with the fact that a healer said my birth was under the influence of a curse from and old girlfriend of my father. I began to breathe normally, and they were going deeper into my most negative thought which was "I am not able". Sometimes I would repeat "I am able" while breathing.

At one point they put on the sound of the Aarti, a Sanskrit chant honoring Babaji and suddenly I started getting into a state of total ecstasy, happiness, love, contentment, plenitude, gratitude and completeness. It is hard to put into words a feeling so strong and vivid. I started with slight smiles, the heart getting warm and with so much love, and suddenly I was completely crying, shouting out with an inner feeling of happiness and gratitude for life. I could feel all my cells, my body vibrating as if I was totally plugged in to an electrical grid, receiving a shock of a thousand volts.

I raised my arms and thus I received more energy. It felt and looked like something from Heaven came inside of me through my hands. I followed my intuition in body movements and observed this energy as star shaped, feeling the expansion of my body with such energy. I gave my hands to Sondra and Markus and the translator, willing to share this energy. Sometimes I shouted "It's beautiful. Thank you!" To bring this energy to humanity was what I wanted the most.

I let go completely. It seems that I freed and liberated everything inside of me. I surrendered totally to the experience, living a love I had never experienced before. I felt no fear, no hesitation at any time. It looked like I was in touch with God. If I died at that moment there would be no problem because I had just experienced the presence of God within me. Words simply cannot match that moment. It was the true liberation and rebirth. People later looked at me and they said they felt like crying.

HO'OPONOPONO

It is my great honor and privilege to be able to introduce you to the ancient technique called Ho'oponopono. I truly thank Morrnah Simeona, a supreme kahuna, who trained me in Hawaii to do this process. It is a combination of special Hawaiian prayers and breathing processes and is one of the sweetest, most gentle and beautiful ways I know of to free oneself and purify oneself. It is a surefire way to clear karma from past lives and release emotional and physical attachments to people, places, and things. The purpose of the process is really freedom from bondage. It can correct mistakes and set relationships right. In the modern form that Morrnah brought to us, it is called *Self-Identity Through HO'OPONOPONO (SITH)*. Ho'oponopono is a major Hawaiian gift. The name itself means "setting right what is already right." Like A Course in Miracles, it functions with deep levels of Divine Forgiveness applied to thoughts in our subconscious and conscious mind. Here are some of the ways it can benefit us:

1. It is a system for maintaining good relationships, not only among family, friends, and colleagues but especially for healing difficult relationships.

2. It is a problem-solving process.

3. It can release the negative effects of past and present actions in our lives, by spiritually, mentally, and physically cleansing through the process of repentance, forgiveness and transmutation.

4. It is a process for righting errors and restoring flow and balance.

5. It is a process for making right any stressful relationship in life. All are set free from tensions created in those relationships.

6. It is a process for looking at ourselves to see how we contributed to any particular problem.

7. It is for clearing what is wrong in families—maybe to find out why someone is sick or to find the real cause of the quarrel.

8. It is a very sophisticated method of conflict resolution in which you only need to work on yourself, free of all confrontations.

9. It embraces spiritual truths, thus lending dignity to the process of conflict resolution.

10. It is a problem-solving system that is perfect, because it aligns all aspects of our being in harmony: Divine Creator; spirit; mind; body, or Divine Creator; superconscious mind; conscious mind; subconscious mind.

Everyone who wants to practice Ho'oponopono in the purest form I know must take the two-day course from the Foundation of I, Freedom of the Cosmos, and agree not to give out the book to anyone. It must be directly handed down from the lineage of Morrnah Simeona to the student, so that the power is never diluted. In other words, you have to agree not to share the manual with others or teach the process to others. However, Morrnah entrusted me as a spiritual teacher and I am allowed to perform the process for others (without giving them the book), which I do in some of our trainings.

It is very timely for what we are going through in the world as it covers all bases.

Self-Identity Through HO'OPONOPONO (SITH). You can take the class to learn the process from one of The Foundation of I, Freedom of the Cosmos's certified instructors. Go here to see their worldwide teaching schedule.
(https://www.self-i-dentity-through-hooponopono.com/)

SAYING OR CHANTING THE MANTRA

This was the main protection Babaji gave us when the pandemic began. In fact, we got this instruction from Him the very day they announced there was a pandemic and a great sequester.

He told us to do 10 rounds of the mantra **Om Namah Shivay** on the mala beads in the morning and evening. There are 108 beads on a mala and that would be one round. He said that 10 rounds would protect us always. It was the most important instruction I got from my master to get protection.

Babaji always said that the mantra Om Namah Shivay is the original mantra. He said it is the highest thought that there is in the universe. He said it is "more powerful than the atom bomb," (and the pandemic, of course). Its literal translation is:

"Oh, Lord Shiva, I bow to thee in reverence." (Shiva is that part of God that burns away or destroys our ignorance and negativity.)

This mantra has many meanings:

It also means "Infinite Spirit," "Infinite Being," and "Infinite Manifestation." (So, your positive thoughts manifest more quickly also.) Where can you get something that destroys your negative thoughts and manifests your positive thoughts at the same time? It also means, "Oh Lord, you are my refuge, thy will be done." It also means, "I bow to the God within." Surely one of those statements will have meaning to you.

The word *man-tra* means "mind" (or thought, thinking) and what you put into it. So, a mantra is a sound, and a word, a vibration you put into your mind. If you put an obscene word into you mind it has a certain low vibration and attracts more low vibrational things. If you put a Divine word into your mind, it has a high vibration and attracts higher like-minded things. Reciting a mantra fills your mind with Spirit. It is a science of vibrational ascension using the actual sound of a holy word to uplift you.

The mantra is like nectar, nourishing you. It is like plugging yourself into the Source. It charges you up. It leads to remembering your total union with God. It enlivens your inner consciousness and helps you to overcome suffering. It provides protection as I said and brings you inner peace.

The Divine Name, or the mantra is Divinity. Babaji said God's name is the greatest treasure on earth. Saying or chanting the mantra is one of the best forms of devotion that there is. Repetition of the mantra purifies the heart. You can achieve all things by doing this "japa" (repetitions of the mantra). Japa yoga is the easiest, quickest, safest, surest, and cheapest way of attaining God realization. Take refuge in His name—all troubles, miseries, pains, and sorrows will come to an end. The Divine Name burns out all your karmas and errors. The Name of God is the master key for success in life and Self-realization. God's name, or the mantra, is the foundation of spirituality.

The name of God is the cure for all disease. (This is called Divine Namapathy.) You can take this medicine for curing anything. And you can administer this medicine for others. You do this by sitting at the side of the patient and singing God's name with sincere devotion and faith. Right now, you would have to do it over the internet. We actually do this over ZOOM for friends of ours all over the world. They really appreciate this infusion of energy. We always recite the Divine Mother mantra at the close of all Liberation Breathing sessions. People tell us how powerful it is for them.

The only real doctor is God. There was a case reported where doctors had pronounced the situation hopeless for a patient and they gave up. The patient was not coming out of his coma. The devotees of Babaji took the case into their own hands. They did continuous chanting of the mantra at the bedside without breaks, taking turns for four hours each group. In several days, the patient sat up, perfectly fine and began chanting also.

So obviously the mantra is also a supreme "pick-me-up" in case you are going into gloom, despair, and low energy.

Even if you just listen to the mantra being sung you will experience delight and healing. We recommend Robby Gass's *Om Namah Shivay* that you can find on YouTube. Just google it for a beautiful meditation that lasts about forty-five minutes.

In case you are one of those people who may resist anything that seems foreign or anything like Eastern philosophy or Hindu mysticism, or anything that seems anti-American in tone, let me suggest the following: STAY OPEN. Be willing to see things differently. Be willing to see something that is "different," differently. As I mentioned earlier, the sanatana dharma is a very ancient system of worship out of which sprung the spiritual traditions of many, many subsequent religious practices. We owe in the Western world a great debt to this holy dharma. Its establishment gave precedent to the rise of more familiar religious practices of prayer and adoration we now enjoy in our own heritage of sacred systems of worship. We try to look at what works for us. We don't even write about what doesn't work. We are interested in results. We also only share with you what will bring you pure joy. The reason we recite a mantra in Sanskrit is because that was the original language, and it is more powerful to do it like that.

MEDITATION

Meditation cannot be done by thinking. Nor does meditation mean making your mind go blank. It is not a kind of self-hypnosis or suggestibility. It has nothing to do with the occult either. There are many schools of meditation, and one can get very befuddled as to which school to practice.

In some schools, meditation might be called a systematic technique for attending to and taking hold of our latent mental power. It might simply be a method of jumping into the subconscious. It does consist of training the mind so that you can go from the surface level of consciousness into the very depths.

Some teachers of meditation believe in order to jump there without thinking, to come to a silent mind, a device is needed. This device will push you to the unknown. The device is an artificial trick to put your rational mind at ease. Sufis used dance as the technique. Zen teachers used koans (puzzles). Rajneesh used a vigorous method called chaotic meditation with catharsis.

Maharishi used a personal mantra that you are given by the instructor, which you say silently to yourself. This was called transcendental meditation (TM). That method has been scientifically proven to produce rejuvenation.

You can make up your own *music meditations.*

In his book *Practical Spirituality*, John Randolph Price defines meditation as follows: "A relaxing of the body, a stilling of emotions, and a narrowing of attention so that the mind may contemplate the inner reality and move into another dimension in consciousness. It is a gentle raising of vibrations so that one may come into alignment with the spiritual self."

He goes on to mention the benefits:

- ❖ Meditation will alleviate stress
- ❖ Reduce high blood pressure
- ❖ Increase resistance to disease
- ❖ Increase the autonomic stability of the nervous system
- ❖ Improve the power of concentration
- ❖ Tap deep reserves of intelligence
- ❖ Contribute to mental clarity
- ❖ Stabilize emotions
- ❖ Improve human relations
- ❖ Relieve insomnia
- ❖ Improve coordination of mind and body
- ❖ Increase learning ability
- ❖ Boost creativity

What if the best meditation did not have a school or a technique? I met a man once who was exploring early methods of photography that captured the first identifiable pictures of babies in the womb. I asked him if he ever meditated? He said, "I am always in a meditation."

What you give your attention to, in this view, is meditation. And what you give your attention to passionately, with single-mindedness, is even greater meditation. And if you are lucky to go all the way and come to the still mind, where the space between your thoughts has widened enough that you are more with the space than with the thoughts, I would say you are really getting somewhere.

The simplest meditation is to just be attentive to your thoughts and the environment around you. This interplay is what you observe. It is a quality of attention more than anything else. It is an appreciation of beauty that goes far beyond any self-imposed technique you may employ to meditate. It is a unification of all your senses cleansed of any judgments or projections. It is the art of *just being*, without the need for anything to be different than it is.

Painting a painting is a meditation. Cooking a good meal is a meditation. Writing a book is a meditation. Observing a friend's face is a meditation. The second you want to isolate your attention with any form of concentration, you have imposed upon yourself a kind of straight jacket of thought that will deny you the very benefits you are trying to achieve—which is freedom from all effort, all pain, all unfulfillment, all doubt, and all conflict.

There is a danger that the very technique for meditation used to liberate you from thought is actually keeping you bound to it. Can you give attention to the present without a technique? Meditation is simply the quality of your attention and does not need a technique. Techniques may be good in the beginning, but you might outgrow them.

If you would like to dedicate a specific time for meditation, then keep it very simple. Sit up erect in a chair with your spine straight. Observe your own thoughts for starters. Don't be so concerned with where they are going or where they have been. Just watch them come and go. Then after a while, observe the space between your thoughts. Gradually this space becomes wider. Keep giving your thought attention until you are more with the space than with the thoughts. This is the simplest way to meditate. It is also what we encourage people to do in a Liberation Breathing session. Just observe your mind and the content of it. Look at it as a whole and let go of the whole thing as an action of meditation. Forgive everyone and everything, including yourself. Don't hold on to a thing. In this letting go is meditation. It is the opposite of concentration or focus.

FASTING

People usually think that fasting is hard and boring. I'd like to offer you another approach—it can be fun and easy. First you must let go of all your belief systems about it. Be willing to see it differently. As with anything, your experience of fasting will depend upon what your thoughts about it are. If you think it will be difficult, it probably will be. It would be good to give up the thought, "I need three meals a day to survive."

Did you know that there are people who eat almost nothing at all? They live on the light of God. There are actual breatharians and we have met one. There is a lesson in A Course in Miracles that goes like this: "I am sustained by the love of God." You need to read that lesson to get over fear of not eating. By the way, fasting is frequently mentioned in the Bible. It *is* a good way of loving God because you are purifying your body and can therefore channel much more of God's love and energy. You can do better at everything.

When we have fasted for a period, we have always received tremendous spiritual rewards and surprises. This is not a reason for doing it, but rather a by-product of the purity obtained.

You can begin easily by fasting on juice one day a week. Then increase it to two days on occasion. We think it is good to go for five days to get more out of it. Mostly the first and second days are the hardest. After that you start cruising! You start to then forget about food and begin to experience the lack of desire to eat. This is when it becomes fun and interesting. Do not deny yourself the pleasure of this experience.

It is easier if you are not doing your usual work routine. If you would like to read about different types of fasts, I recommend the book *Are You Confused?* You could start on the Master Cleanser fast, which is a drink made of pure water, lemon juice, maple syrup and cayenne pepper. You can carry this with you all day. On this fast, you really don't get hungry.

Another good fast is to simply drink fresh juices.

Babaji told me to give up food for a period of time. The longest I lasted was 30 days. I did not get hungry, but I got angry. That is why Babaji for sure suggested it. He told me to walk a lot then.

Fasting to lose weight is not so good really. It is better to fast for spiritual reasons and then it seems like a reward instead of a punishment. Sometimes a guru will recommend you fast every Monday for example. Your body will tell you when you need to fast.

If one person in a family begins to clean up this way, the rest of the family is automatically affected. You begin to move a lot of energy and you will see the results around you.

FIRE PURIFICATION

Fire purification is an ancient technique for clearing one's aura and one's karma. It is also good for releasing anger, guilt, and so on. It is quite simple. All you have to do is meditate on the fire with your eyes open. This can be done with a fireplace, an open bonfire, or lacking these, even a candle. Meditate on the fire at the level of the navel to gain immense strength.

Babaji taught us to meditate on the elements. He also taught us the ancient fire ceremony where you feed the fire with fruits, grains, incense, and flowers to return your gratitude to the Source. Prayers and mantras are recited by a high priest during this ceremony, which if done properly is also a ceremony for world peace.

Babaji said, "Worshipping the fire means worshipping the inner light. Worshipping the fire burns karma. It is spiritual purification. Worshipping the fire transforms into pure love all that is impure in the heart and mind. From the power of the holy fire, the flame of love unfolds the qualities of the soul."

MUNDAN

Mundan is a complete shaving of the head. It is an initiation rite. For Markus and me, we did it to be initiated into the Babaji-Divine Mother lineage. We did it again when we got married. Once we did it for an entire year and shaved each other's heads. Very special! When you do it correctly, especially along the Ganges, Babaji commits to lead you all the way to liberation.

Besides liberation there are many other benefits:

❖ It opens your crown chakra
❖ Gives you deep inner peace
❖ Processes your birth trauma
❖ Processes your past life karma
❖ Helps you let go of old mental and physical patterns
❖ Shifts your energy completely
❖ Represents sacrifice of the superficial
❖ Brings healing to the body
❖ Brings a spiritual rebirth
❖ Makes you a lot more creative
❖ Gets you over what other people think
❖ Processes out your fear of cults
❖ Opens up angelic channels

CREATIVE WRITING

Markus is always writing in some journal. This is a spiritual purification practice for him. He gets in a state of inner emptiness and asks the muse of creativity to come through him. His *Odes to the Divine Mother* (https://bit.ly/OdesRay) he wrote in this way over a period of four years on the road. He wrote a little fable here explaining why spiritual purification is necessary.

In a time eons ago, a native Son of the Cosmos came down to planet earth from the Great Family of Light Beings. There was a burst of Pure Joy that covered the earth as a result of His arrival. The Light was taking shape into a body, and the body participated in the great diversity of Life. The trees and the rivers all welcomed Him. The animals and the birds looked toward His Light for peace and inspiration. All were blessed by His presence on earth. All the diversity of Life was very grateful that their Creator had sent such a beautiful Light Being into their midst. What was "unseen" before was now "seen." It was as if God came down incarnate. All the entities of planet earth experienced this Joy. Even the rocks had great reverence for Him, as He did for them. The stillness they had for eons was infused with a new dynamism. Even in their absolute stillness the rocks and mountains that seemed so immovable were now moved. They were moved, even in their stillness, by a Pure Joy never before experienced. They were so proud to not move, or go anywhere, except by such slow and infinitesimal erosions of what seemed like time. But with this coming of the Great Light of the native Son, they had certainty now in their Being, which was immortal. Even in the grains of sand, trillions upon trillions put together making up the mountains, they could rejoice in the perpetual Happiness of all that they were. All this, the Native Son of the Light brought to them. It was absolutely miraculous. All things on earth participated in this Great Celebration of Truth, of Joy, of Gratitude to be Alive.

At some point the Great Mother of the Universe, the One responsible for all physical manifestations of the whole Cosmos, sent down a manifestation of Herself, just as the Father of the Light had done before with Her collaboration, to send the Native Son. She sent her Holy Daughter as Herself. She was the epitome of Beauty, of Grace, of Giving, of Absolute Love and Care. Together these two beings of the Great Light and the Great Cosmic Manifestation of the Divine Mother peopled the earth. There was a Unity in all. There was a Union on all levels of being. The Great Spirit of the Light, the Great Mind and Body of the Cosmic Mother, all came together in this holy Union. The perfect Yoga was born, and all entities on the planet took their Joy and added to it. Joy upon Joy was increased. Joy upon Joy was combined together in new possibilities of Great Love. Joy upon Joy was the Light emanating out from the planet earth to the rest of the Cosmos. GOD's GREAT EXPERIMENT was working nicely. There was a Divine Quality that was experienced by everything here on earth, everywhere. Peace and Joy abounded, extended and thrived. The Divine Mother and the Divine Father were made manifest and Their Will was for perfect happiness for all their creations to increase, extend and abound.

Earth was such a wondrous place to be! Immortality was certain. And, the Sons and Daughters of the Light could come and go anytime. They could manifest from the Light, and they could return to the Light at will, disembodied from the physical realms. They had the ability to materialize and dematerialize at will. It was a great joy to have this Freedom, because they knew they were Immortal Beings of Light and Love and Joy. They could be all of these—in a body or out of a body. They were certain there was no difference. Yet, the entities of the Earth became attached to them. They knew their Life of diversity had been unified by the Presence of these Light Beings. They knew that in the Presence of these Beings here on earth was one of Pure Joy. When a Native Son or Daughter of the Light went back to the Cosmos, they became sad. They could not "see them" anymore. They could not feel them, it seemed. All they could see was a "pile of dust," or a "remembrance of things past."

There were lots of Light Beings who came to planet Earth. But gradually, the entities of the Earth, and even the Light Beings themselves, forgot Who they were. The things of this Life in a body forgot about the Life of the Light, of the non-physical Spirit realms. Gradually this Light of the Spirit, whose SOURCE was Pure Joy, and whose Presence on Planet Earth was an embodiment of this Pure Joy, was forgotten. Without this Joy the birds felt homeless, and they flew about always searching for a new place to nest. The fish in the sea hid in the dark, lurking places, in fear of the larger fish

47

who wanted to eat them. The gazelles became faster and faster on their feet, to avoid their dramatic end in the jaws of the cunning cats. And even the Beings of the Light began to congregate in groups, and speak in different tongues, and consider themselves "different" from other Beings of the Light, and to have dominion over certain "territories" they called their own. And these groups began to compete for the most Beautiful and Fertile Manifestations of the Divine Mother, just like the biggest elephants became the sires of the most beautiful and fertile mother elephants.

Time entered in. One age supplanted another age. One dominant Being of the Light replaced another, until no one remembered they all came here from the same Source of One Great Light. The dominant Beings ruled over the less dominant Beings. Violence and control, not Love and compassion, ruled the day. Greed entered in. The dominators wanted more from the dominated, and from the Mother's Earth. And through their cleverness they obtained it, often without the dominated Beings even knowing how it happened. But often they did know it. Some Beings of the Light were enslaved by those more dominant Beings of the Light. Life on earth was no longer one of Pure Joy. It was a struggle for survival. It was a land of substitutions. The Bliss of the Light, and the Pure Joy imparted by the Original Light Beings on earth was replaced with the accumulations of ownership and resources. The Dominant Beings of the Light made great kingdoms of wealth and apparent glory. They ruled by what they called "divine right," but it was a sham, a substitute for the True Rulership of the Light, of the Love that brought the Light Beings to planet earth in the first place. What a mess it became. What had been a place of Pure Joy, singing to the Whole Universe of this Heaven on Earth, became a "hell on earth." What was Pure Joy when the original Beings of the Light came here, was now a pit of sorrow. The Beings of the Light forgot that they are Immortal, they forgot they are Joined and connected to everything in Creation through this Light. They forgot that reemerging into the Spirit realms of the non-physical dimension of the Light is just as alive as being manifested in a body in this physical dimension of the Light. They got attached to this dimension. They lost their Pure Joy.

So this is why Spiritual Purification is necessary. Simply put, it is a practice of remembering who we are as Beings of the Light. It is the means we use to remember Who we are as God Created us. It is the waking up from a deep sleep of amnesia that has gone on for eons. It is the practice of remembering the Original Pure Joy we felt when we were there with the first Being of the Light Who descended to earth. It is our remembrance of Wholeness, Perfect Happiness we shared with the Rocks, Mountains, Trees, Oceans, Plants and Animals that were already here on earth, who were experiencing the Pure Joy of the Cosmic Light of the Divine Father, Mother and Child as ONE! Spiritual Purification is necessary so we can experience the Pure Joy of miracles, of being the Light Itself. We endeavor to remember what was always there in our Being— the Infinite Source of Light that we are.

SOME OTHER SPIRITUAL PRACTICES

Silence—Spend some time by yourself. Just listen to the sounds around you, without any distractions. Be present without "doing."

Sleep Reduction—Wake up a couple hours earlier than your normal routine. Take a walk before the sun comes up. Notice how much more you get done with your day.

Body Work—This is a wide range of things. I like Rolfing which is deep tissue work that rearranges the facia, the connecting tissue between the muscle system. Whatever it is, you must make sure you have a good connection to whoever you allow to lay hands upon you. Their energy is very important. You have to totally trust them.

Colonics—Markus and I have colonic irrigation board. This is a home colonic board that you can set up easily in your bathroom, with a five-gallon container and tube that gives you a very effective home colonic.

We do a few rounds of these colonics a couple time a year to keep our colons detoxed.

Float to Relax Tanks—I have done this a few times in my life. It was very hallucinatory. I thought there was a guy in there with me, although there wasn't. So, it was very powerful, to say the least. And it helped me see the power of the mind to project its own reality.

Yoga, Tai Chi, etc.—Markus did Kundalini Yoga with Yogi Bhajan in the 1980s in his younger years, and this is what eventually led him to Rebirthing and A Course in Miracles. Yoga is a life-long spiritual practice and there are many facets to it. Vivekananda, a disciple of Sri Ramakrishna, the first yogi to bring Vedanta to the West (long before Yogananda) wrote the clearest modern-day treatises on all different forms of yoga.

Celibacy—I have been celibate in different periods of my life. So, this is not a problem for me. But neither do I see anything less spiritual by having a good sex life. When Markus and I got together in 2008 celibacy was something we decided was not necessary for our soul evolution. In fact, sacred sexuality is just as powerful a practice in our spiritual repertoire. So, this is what we practice now.

International Travel to Sacred Sites—International travel in general clears a person of a lot of past-life karma with lives in those other countries. And travel to specifically charged up sites in foreign lands, and even in your own country, can hugely forward you in your spiritual growth. We take groups to India, Bali, Iceland, Glastonbury, Ecuador, and any place that the vibe is high. We go to New Mexico twice a year to charge up as well.

Journaling—Writing down your thoughts is a discipline we all should nurture. It gets you clear. It helps you stay in the flow of engagement with life. A person who writes down their thoughts can also know themselves better. I have always written. And now we have so many mediums in which we can all do this. As we mentioned for the gratitude journal, get a nice blank book that inspires you and just start writing down your thoughts.

Here's the Glitch

Some people say they don't have time to do purification techniques, yet you can get a lot more done in a shorter period of time when you are clear. It used to take over a year for us to write a book. Now it goes so much faster because we are clearer. These practices are the best investments you can make in yourself. Your work will improve, and you will even make more money. And you will be more often in a state of pure joy. These are just a few of the ones we practice. You may discover your own if you give attention to your spiritual awakening in *The Supermarket for a Meaningful Life.*

 **#5.**

AN AISLE FOR ART & CULTURE

SPIRITUAL POETRY

Poets have very exalted thoughts in general, and if a poet is writing spiritual poetry, it is something very, very special for you. You can be taken to a new and higher dimension from which that poetry came. Spiritual poetry is like alchemy on the body, especially if read aloud. It comes from a place that not only raises your vibrations but can actually make your DNA more orderly because it is always about the poet's love for God and about the love of God coming back down in a form of special energy for you.

This kind of poetry inspires you to have a new way of thinking. When you have a new way of thinking, the old habitual, boring thoughts to which one might be addicted are erased. It should always be a goal to free your mind from habitual negative thinking. A spiritual poet helps you do that.

Spiritual poetry helps you get closer to God and that is exactly what we need to do in a time of crisis. Anytime you get closer to God, you get better in every way. Old habits drop away, and you feel great, and you get more protection from the negative influences in life. A spiritual poet can literally get you into a different part of your mind. This, in fact, makes you more creative yourself. Notice what happens after you read poetry and what you feel like doing as a result.

A great spiritual poet gets you closer to the truth because he is not coming from his ego. One could never write spiritual poetry from the ego. The ego is a false self that we made up to replace God. It is a combination of all your negative thoughts that keep you from remembering God. It is an idol. It is the cause of all your pain and suffering and despair. To be enlightened, one has to replace the ego with the Holy Spirit's thought system. This is what a poet helps us do. Spiritual poetry can lead you to enlightenment.

This kind of poetry takes you to a place above your problems. Sometimes you get stuck in a problem and you just cannot get the solution because your mind itself is stuck. That is when you need to do something different. At a time like that, it is best to do some kind of spiritual practice—such as Liberation Breathing, chanting, praying, singing, or reading poetry. You may not be the kind that is used to reading poetry. Well, I suggest you just try it anyway.

When you read spiritual poetry, a peace can come over you, if you are not in resistance. Our goal should be peace. A spiritual poet has quieted his mind; that ordinary chatter is gone. He can hear the celestial voice and download the state of peace with his words. I have always seen that when Markus writes poetry—his mind is closer to the state of empty. That is where creativity happens. The poet erases before he gets to that state.

You can be refreshed when you read spiritual poetry. Sometimes you feel down, fatigued, or even exhausted from certain situations. You need a way to refresh yourself. Poetry is like taking a shower. Taking several showers a day even if you did not get dirty, is a good idea because you clear your energy system, which can get polluted. So, imagine taking a shower and reading spiritual poetry after that. It is a double refresher. Spiritual poetry can have a youth giving effect on your body. Try it and notice it. Get your mind washed.

Spiritual poetry can inspire you. It opens you up to getting that flash of intuition you need. Anything that sharpens your intuition should be something you want to have for yourself. It is a gift you are giving to yourself. When you read Markus's poetry, you are giving a gift to yourself. His presence, his love, his vibration, and his words will soothe you and inspire you.

Spiritual poetry like this helps you love life more. The poet is in love with life already. He is already there. Spiritual poetry is all about God and God is all about life—and life is the highest force in the universe. When you love life with a passion, life works with you. Life gives you an incredible ride. Everything becomes like an amusement park!

Spiritual poetry can make you more abundant. It is coming from a place of opulence because that is what God is. God is opulent. Opulence becomes your normal state when you hang around the masters or sit in their vibration. Spiritual poetry is like a blooming rose bush, a fertile forest, and a grand fiesta of abundant love. Think abundance all around you. Spiritual poetry can do that.

Through Markus's poetry you can gain an understanding of who the Divine Mother is at a deeper level. She is not just a Hindu goddess with eight arms and a blue body; She is so far beyond all that. It takes a spiritual poet to take us to the level from which the Divine Mother comes, to give us a glimpse of who the Divine Mother really is—to bring you the energy of the Divine Mother Herself. And it is a real gift to receive the energy of the Divine Mother Herself and transmit it through words! I am happy that you are willing to receive this gift.

I feel so lucky because Markus has been memorizing some of his poems and he recites them aloud for practice. I get to hear these praises right here at home.

Here are some of my favorites:

"My Knock That Yearns For Heaven"

Would the door of Your Love be opened by my knock that yearns for Heaven in the part of my deepest desire? What is this peace and joy you promise as my sure inheritance? Your grace is given me to claim now in this ocean of joy you bestow on me. Let me knock my last knock as You open this door of Your love to my total eternity. Why would I delay one second more in those regions bereft of full awareness, in those lands of unfulfilled desires that lie languishing in the sands of time? You open the portal that I may enter now into this present moment of pure release. No more would I await Your Love for future days. The future is now, and the past of all shortcomings done. Here I am Divine Mother of this doorway to compassion. I step through this opening to a different world, never to return to doubt and despair. You are my cause for being, to where I would return, never having left in truth. You are my cause for rejoicing in this moment of total liberation. I ask and it is given. I knock and doors are opened by Your absolute love for me. I claim it now in the blazing truth of gratitude for all that lives in me, a life I share with everything seen and unseen. Now the door of Your Love is open for my love to pour through and meld with You forever.

"In This Kitchen of Your Love"

In this kitchen of your love, all are fed. We are blessed in the Presence of your holy hands that prepare the food so carefully and infuse each morsel of nourishment with the promise of good health and longevity. Divine Mother of all who are hungry for Your Love, let me work in the kitchen of this holy sustenance. Give me a task of preparation for the dish of this divine banquet. Let me serve those who come to eat in this hallowed hall of holiness at the table of total satisfaction. I observe the people who you feed and fill to the very brim of their soul. I see the compassion of Your total mercy to accept each one exactly as he is in the innocence of his truest nature. You quench the thirst of our deepest need for the nectar of immortality. You wipe away the urge for death to end a life gone awry by thoughts of lack and limitation. Take from all the hunger of despair and feed them with the cornucopia of compassion. I serve in the kitchen of Your Love a meal so complete that one bite is equal to a thousand feasts of former lives partaken. Bring this food to the table of a holy communion and infuse each guest with the wine of eternal life. Give them the bread they so much desire, a certain care from Your never-ending Providence.

"A Sliver of Your Light"

A sliver of Your Light is all I can stand. A small glimmer of Your Reality comes close to my eyes, and I am almost blinded by its brilliance. Little by little I can look more upon Your creation with the awe of a joyous child who sees the endless possibilities of his play. You protect me from harm and show me the flowers of Your constellations, the blooms of Andromeda and Orion in the garden of a galaxy of stars. From the heavens this thin ray of light comes so swiftly toward me, yet for so many years it travelled through space to reach my innocent eyes—my observations unexplainable, so vast are their proportions. I am attuned with You now; my body, soul, and might, aligned with Your loving care that I may be like You as Your Son, immortal in my ways of service to the rest of Your creation. You give me meaning in a world of no meaning. In that arena of struggle and strife, sickness and death, You place me in the middle of illusions to overcome the sorrow of a tired humanity that has forgotten You. With this small glimmer of Your brilliance, I am illuminated forever, to extend Your gentle embrace of a Mother to all. This light of Love exceeds my expectations. Only a sliver is all I need to enlighten my Self, the Son of Your own Identity.

One of the greatest gifts in the Aisle of Art and Culture is to give attention to other cultures around the world. Traveling is the best way to see these cultures first-hand and experience their similarities and differences. We go to India every year to recharge our spiritual batteries and to expand our consciousness in ways that could not be expanded any other way. I have travelled to India over 45 times since 1977. In India we sing praises to the Divine Mother such as this:

Oh, Sivai, You are the embodiment of ultimate bliss and conscious energy. You are supreme knowledge of the Absolute. You are the image of infinite compassion, unfathomable as is the deep sea. Oh Durga, Goddess of the universe, I prostrate before you.

Oh Universal Mother, you give me shelter. In truth, You are the one who gives life to all the beings of this world. You are the physician who cures the fever of the life cycles on this wheel of life. You are the source of life and liberation to all living beings. Remembering You is to crown this life with success, to attain liberation.

You are the embodiment of divine speech and hidden supreme knowledge. You are the embodiment of the initial seed of OM and are rooted therein. You are the energy of Kundalini, giving birth to creation. The knowledge of You in this divine form enables the yogis no more to return to the mother's womb.

Markus on Art

I have written a blog on art for eight years now. It is called

ART LOOK—an art lover's companion—
https://markusray.com/art-look/

There are many articles on various artists, articles on my own art, and art of the masters who I admire. You can read more there than I could possibly write about in this book, but I feel a few big points about art need to be said here. I did my formal art study at the Cleveland Institute of Art back in the 1970s, and Tyler School of Art of Temple University in Philadelphia in the 1980s, ending up with an MFA in painting, drawing, and sculpture. I have been painting and drawing ever since then. Art has been in my blood and in my breath, which is where it originates.

Tara Singh, my master teacher of A Course in Miracles, said, "The only *art* is the *art of living*." This could also be called the art of loving—of holy relationships, of our relationship to life itself, to the Source of Creation, to our fellow humans, to the whole of this cosmos—this is the only ART. He was very well versed in the arts. He knew about painting, sculpture, architecture, music, dance, drama, and the plastic arts. Yet he was certain that the human being came first, and all art is meant to uplift mankind into greater realms of the spirit, into a state of pure joy, into wholeness. He transformed my life. He did that. He lifted me into a state of pure joy. He was my master. He was my friend. He was my liberator. He was my secret sharer. He was my destroyer of illusions. He was my illuminator. He was my holy companion. He was my teacher of the highest art possible. He was my everything.

Art and culture are important. Yet, seeing with the still mind and the silent mind would be the beginning of this culture of creativity. Tara Singh would say, out of this space comes "the voice that precedes thought." And this is true inspiration, the source for all cultural creativity, all forms of art, and all of life itself. I have invoked this stillness and silence into my works. Everything I write, everything I create comes from this "art of living" I learned from Tara Singh. I am lucky.

Here is an article I wrote on Tintoretto's paintings at the National Gallery last year, just down the street from us in Washington DC, to show you what I mean:

Tintoretto's Genius Shut Me Up!

Dear Readers, I have been absent from ART LOOK, though not absent from looking—or writing. I apologize for this hiatus. My writing priorities were applied to getting two books together for Sondra and me: *Lately I've Been Thinking,* two years of her Facebook Posts consolidated in a compendium of tidbits of wisdom, and *Liberation*, a short manual about the personal lie (the most negative subconscious judgment we have about ourselves) and how to liberate ourselves from it. Those books can be purchased both paperback and e-book at **bit.ly/LatelyRay** and **bit.ly/LibRay** respectively.

But here is the real reason you have not heard from me—on two occasions I sauntered over to the National Gallery to see the Tintoretto Exhibition. I was so blown away by it I was left speechless. Tintoretto's genius shut me up. That's the real reason. I was speechless in the presence of Tintoretto's genius. What could I add or detract, with pen or brush, to the huge pile of human endeavors to create the sublime? Tintoretto "shut me the fuck up" and I am hardly recovered from the silencing.

Well, passions are possible to move us again. I am moved to write an Art Look, after a long period of digestion. Three tours of duty later, I find myself in Curitiba, Brazil, looking back on my many months of pondering the power of the things I saw. Truly I was moved. And so can you be, looking at this glimpse of what has taken me five months to fathom.

When going through such a major exhibit as this, in a world class museum, there is so much to take in. Coupled with the fact that Tintoretto is one of the "gods" of high Italian Renaissance painting mastery, I could only be humbled at the very least. But then, inspiration comes after the shock of it all. There are paintings that move me more than others. There are artists that move me more than others. Plenty of great painters came out of Venice in the 15th and 16th centuries, but Tintoretto is one of my guiding lights. He is the one I remember. And of his works in the National Gallery, I discuss a few here.

I will do my best to give insights into those—"the ones that moved me the most." These are like the jewels in the crown of Tintoretto's genius. He was painting and feeling like no other in his times. There is an X-factor in his work that creates an atmosphere of the "other worldly," but at the same time is very grounded in the flesh and bones of this corporeal dimension. They "moved me," not just because of their formal prowess, but because they capture a Spiritual Truth that transcends the physicality of what we actually see in them. They transmit a silence that rises above the world, but at the same time they play a symphony of visual truth that fills our vision with unbelievable human delight.

The One that Moved Me the Most

Baptism of Christ

This painting is about 15 feet tall, larger than life. It towered over me. I could hardly believe human hands painted such a thing. I could hardly imagine that this one moment in time, the holiest of holiest, could be captured in paint. What would this creation have taken, in the man who painted it? What true connection to his Source would this action have required of his reservoir of painterly and spiritual wisdom to coalesce at once in his genius? And, from the Source of this Holy Instant, how did he benefit himself from giving the ages a true view into this miraculous event? I am not in a position to say. But it is obvious that Tintoretto had this connection. Without it this painting would not have come into being through his hands—literally being used by the Hands of God.

The Holy Spirit

One can acknowledge symbolism, and this is okay. All painters must contend with this necessity of symbolism. The descending dove and the light rays of the Holy Spirit are strongly placed. They are prominent elements of the picture. Well, okay. We make the leap of faith to accept that the symbol and the meaning of the symbol are close to one and the same. How would you paint the Holy Spirit? It is formless, shapeless, timeless, edgeless, and spaceless. But you have to give it some form. So, okay. The dove has been it—the object of flight downward of a Cosmic Energy sent to affirm the better angels of our nature—this is how artists have depicted the Holy Spirit. Let's "dig it," not poo-poo it as pictorial fantasy.

The Master of Diagonals

Tintoretto mastered the diagonal as an ordering of his dynamics. No other painter in history so employed the diagonal to compose pictures and capture the movement of our hearts and minds. He leads us through his vision as though we are on a journey to Nirvana—and it is his responsibility to insure we reach it.

These two men are intertwined in a drama of deep spiritual dalliance that sets our mind in a kind of trance. The diagonals lead us through the drama, and make sure we grasp the whole thing in our six seconds of attention. The light is focused strongly around the head of the Christ in His total surrender, with head bowed down in anticipation of his "journey into the dark." And this is what the Great Renaissance was all about—a rebirth of the spirit into the otherwise darkness of the Middle Ages. It was a triumph of humanism and classical trust in the ascendency of man's greater good in an otherwise feudal and oppressive social system.

The diagonal, rather than a detour of vectors off track from the church norm of perpendicular rigidity, becomes a holy salvation in Tintoretto's compositions. They weave us through the space and open up a dimension in us, far greater than the perimeters of the picture plane.

They take us into Divine Space, which is boundless in its potential to awaken us to a higher reality.

A son of a fabric dyer, Tintoretto elevated himself from the lowly craft trades of his father's class into the rarified moment of Holy Encounter—

Baptism's Diagonals

and attained the means of expression and observation unsurpassed in the Venetian Schools of painting. Not even Titian, his elder and more famous counterpart, had the raw talent of his brief student. Tintoretto's father enrolled his son in Titian's studio as an apprentice. Legend has it that the boy's drawings were so dynamic and enthralling that Titian, jealous of the young man's natural genius, sent him home in an act of excommunication from fear of being outshined. Titian gave Tintoretto the cold shoulder his entire life. That tells you something right there as to the genius of Tintoretto, the "dyer's son."

The Last Supper

Most of us who have looked at art know *The Last Supper* by Leonardo Da Vinci. It is a very balanced image, with perfect one-point perspective, converging in the middle with Christ's head taking on major importance in the centralized, symmetrical view of the Idealized Savior. Tintoretto's version is a more *rough and tumble* picture, and the dynamism of the figures create a dramatic whirlwind of activity swirling around the off center version of the Christ.

The Last Supper

"Reach for the flask of wine, Brother James, and Yo, buddy, knock over a few chairs in the revelry of your inebriation!" Don't cha wanna be there! It's a kind of fun fest flaunted in the face of proper church protocol, taken down from the Altars of respectability and put in the back rooms of our ebullient blasts of bromance. If the theme were not so serious, we would perhaps mistake it for a pre-nuptial stag party.

Again, the diagonals, vectoring left and right, plummet our eyes all over the place, to take in the fullness of the scene. You have people falling all over the place here. It is as if the figures are just pieces in a greater scheme of compositional bombast. Some of the disciples are watchful and attentive, but some are obviously in a drunken stupor, it seems, falling to the left, leaning to the right, in a kind of mime to get the right diagonal piece in a conglomerate of a sacred but dynamic picture puzzle. Tintoretto is not only the master of the diagonal, he is a master of the religious drama he is making clear to the public. His devotion goes beyond the acceptable canons of a polite and ordered Last Supper, into the flesh and blood content of an actual happening. If Tintoretto was a photo journalist, he would be the one getting the "picture of the year," taken amidst the heart of the most dramatic event of the day.

Last Supper Diagonals

The Nine Muses

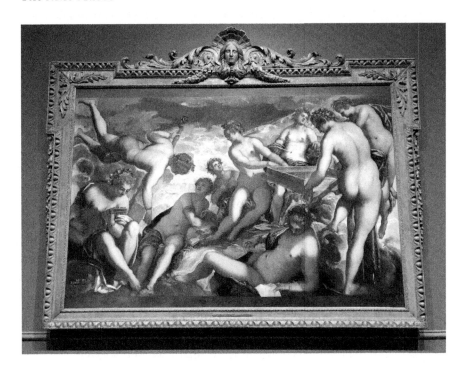

The Nine Muses

The Nine Muses have inspired artists for centuries. Tintoretto made them his subject in this painting. Mythology has it that they are the daughters of Zeus, King of the Gods, and Mnemosyne, the Titan Goddess of Memory. They all have very definite functions to inspire science, arts, drama, poetry, and all the highest cultural creations. Here is the list of them: Calliope (Muse of Epic Poetry); Clio (Muse of History); Erato (Muse of Love Poetry); Euterpe (Muse of Music and Song); Melpomene (Muse of Tragedy); Polyhymnia (Muse of Hymns); Terpsichore (Muse of Dance); Thalia (Muse of Comedy); Urania (Muse of Astronomy).

Not that you have to know these names particularly to get the power of this painting. It is a "tight space," in my opinion, in which Tintoretto packs the ultimate drama of the female form. Placed in a kind of harem of high culture that suggests the greater functions of women, even the

Divine Mother, these muses lead the creative person through the paces that ultimately result in very particular expressions. The muse is a spark, an inspiration, a "thought in the mind of God," which comes down and into the artist as a kind of super food. The Food of inspiration is then transformed in the creative crucible of Tintoretto's skill to paint his way into the annals of art history, in the broader sense, but into the guts of ourselves, in the visceral view of what is actually before us.

Mind you, this is all before photography. The touch of the artist's hand is upon all of those limbs, and he must put them together in the wholeness of a Truth so poignant that we are transfixed. One can hardly take his eyes off this work in its actual presence. And again, his diagonals spread our vision across the multitude of all his painterly strokes, giving us a view of space that is timeless and boundless. One is not the same after seeing this painting in person.

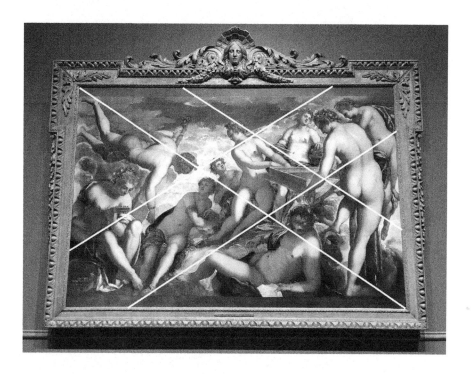

The Diagonals of the Nine Muses

The Precursor of El Greco

Art builds on what came before it. Tintoretto built on Titian who was 28 years his senior. Though Titian may loom larger in the annals of art history than Tintoretto, in my book the younger was his "better." There is a holy presence in Tintoretto that Titian may lack. This could just be my opinion, without academic grounding to make this claim. But at the same time, I cannot take my eyes off Tintoretto's works. When I say I was rendered speechless, I really mean that. I could hardly think about writing "about" his work after it entered my very heart and soul. It truly silenced my thought.

Holy Mother and Christ Child

This *Holy Mother and Christ Child* is stunning. Granted, it is in the context of Tintoretto's patrons who financed the work, but the crux of the peace and joy transmitted, along with the "musical boys" chirping into the general elation of the scene, melts my heart and lifts my soul into realms hitherto unfelt. Only blessings ensue and pour out of their hand gestures of sacred touching. The larger view does not add nor detract from the central core of this work. The patrons have their prime-time space wearing their rich raiment of ermine and velvet. The priests get their cameo appearance in their stiff collared worship of the Holy Mother and Child. Tintoretto creates a pyramid of perfection with his adoration of the diagonal. We are brought to the pinnacle of perfection in the holding out of holiness. This is not a mere holiness of church dogma or belief, but a profound meeting with beauty and balance. With all the vectors flying here and there in the compositions of these master works, the artist never forgets we are most likely moved by the harmony of his elements all rolled into a kind of visual music. He even elevates the *Boys of Music* to the status of angels—by giving them wings. Bet you didn't notice that.

Holy Mother and Christ Child with diagonals

Art builds on what came before it. The chiaroscuro of Titian underlies the genius of Tintoretto's tonal virtuosity. He is a master of light and dark, shadow and brilliance, foreshortening, and contrapposto. He is a colorist and a structuralist altogether. He is a mystic and a visionary above even a master craftsman. Why would younger artists not flee to him for guidance?

El Greco's Holy Mother with the Christ Child

and solace? Tintoretto is a safe haven for our souls. He lifts us in moments we need lifting. He soothes us in the midst of a movement that is almost overwhelming. And it is this upon which the later artist, El Greco, strongly built. That is the subject for another Art Look, but at least for now we can see the influence Tintoretto had on great artists yet to come—El Greco being one of them.

The dynamic lessons of Tintoretto's diagonals were indelibly drawn to stay. El Greco took these lessons to heart. Twenty-three years younger than Tintoretto, El Greco took up the baton in the relay team to pictorial Truth, or the sacred brush in this case, to carry on the dynamism of Tintoretto's legacy. Figure this one out yourself. You don't need a red-lined diagram from me to see the similar use of the diagonal to crisscross our attention toward the beautiful elements that matter. The Mother sits adoring the epitome of adoration—The Christ. Youth and angels aside, we are moved into a heavenly realm. Who cares if they are "floating on clouds" ascending, and we cannot make that modern leap into iconic and symbolic reality? There is something beyond the realms of what can be verified by science and the senses. We can be enlightened into spiritual dimensions that even transcend what the body's eyes perceive. We are still moved by the genius of the vision, nonetheless.

On a Late Summer Day, Looking into the Future

It is a late summer day, here in Curtiba, Brazil, and I am looking into the future. Again, I meant it when I said Tintoretto "shut me up." I had to assess my place, 500 years later, in the scope of those who pick up a brush or a charcoal stick seriously. We are products of our times, of our social and familial conditioning. This is just a fact. We are also the competitors in a challenge to overcome our self- limiting nature. The great artists give us hope and also show us the work yet to be done. The genius of Tintoretto put me in touch with a higher aspiration as yet unreached. But every viewing of great mastery provides a window into our own possibilities for self-mastery. And this is what the five months of silence did to me. Tintoretto upped the stakes in the seriousness of my craft. He infused me with more courage to face myself, but in the process, I had to admit my shortcomings—albeit self-imposed. The wise can change their mind and harness certainty, thank God.

Reclining Muse on a Late Summer Day

It is a late summer day here in Curitiba. I am on the edge of a new life. Only I can limit it. But in Tintoretto, the reclining figure of pure relaxation is the muse that guides me. I look into the future of pure facility. One can do anything they set their Holy Mind to do. And so it is! I am walking a new talk and painting a new dream with Tintoretto behind me; the cloth dyer's son who was originally rejected by the Venetian artistic powers that be.

Who can reject our aspirations but ourselves, in the end? Tintoretto was not thwarted one bit. The rejection gave him fuel to press on. And that we all must do—press on to our highest aspirations. Aspira Astra — "reach for the stars." What is it you want to do? Where do you want to go? And how do you want to do it? These are questions of the heart Tintoretto brought to himself and answered them with his genius. We all have a genius in us that provides the answers. We just need to be clear about the questions. Then in this clarity, may the diagonal meanders of our soul come together in the vectors that point our way. I cannot wait to "paint the next one." I invoke the spirit of Tintoretto's genius to accompany me. And may you do the same. GOD BLESS you guys.

Love,

Markus

Art and Culture are supremely important in *The Supermarket for a Meaningful Life.* We encourage you to get involved with something in the area of these loftier forays of observation, partaking of the creative outpourings that lift our soul to greater awareness of our own Divine Perfection.

Sondra on THE HOLY CULTURE OF HOME

The Altar

One wonderful way to love God is to prepare one or more altars in your home. We were so inspired to do this after visiting Bali where they have temples in their homes and temples everywhere. They would not consider starting a workday without doing prayer rituals at their many altars. The whole family sits down and weaves baskets together every morning in which they put flowers, incense, and other offerings. Then they take this to their workplace and put them on an altar there.

Our main altar in our living room is a beautiful antique rosewood table with Roman columns. On the top we have pictures of Amma, the hugging saint; the Virgin Mary; and a statue of Quan Yin from the Nelson Atkins Museum in Kansas City. On the bottom tier we have our male masters. We actually have an altar in every room. We can tell you how powerful that is: Once I had a huge fire in my apartment building while I was out of town. The walls in the hall were like black tar and the paintings had melted into the walls. The wreath on my front door was melted into the door. All the apartments were destroyed except mine. The building was condemned. And yet, there was not one speck of soot in my apartment. The altars had protected it perfectly.

You might have resistance to an altar if you have not cleared your feelings about religion and any disappointment you have around that subject. To do that, here is a way to clear: Go back to your original church and sit in a pew during the service and breathe a lot, forgiving everything that was confusing and appreciating everything that was helpful.

It does not matter what religion you were raised in. What matters is a reverence and love for God NOW. An altar will help you achieve this reverence, this respect. It will remind you to think holy thoughts during the day and perhaps it will inspire you to do spiritual practices. It will remind you of your absolute connection with the Source. When people come to your home, they too will be inspired and treat you with more respect. We can vouch for that. They will actually appreciate you for reminding them of their love for God.

Often when we have a problem, we write letters to the Dream Team and place these letters under the altar cloth. It ALWAYS works. The problem clears up. Don't forget this. This is how you can write a responsible letter:

Dear Babaji, (or whoever is your deity)

1. This is my problem_____.
2. These are the negative thoughts that created this problem _____ (list them).
3. I lay them at Your feet.
4. These are my new thoughts. (List affirmations that are the opposite of #2.)
5. Please add energy to these new thoughts.
6. Thank You.
7. Signature and date

Prayer

A lot of people have given up on prayer, thinking that they have not received what they asked for. Let's look at the matter in a new way. First of all, if you have asked for something and not received it, maybe you need to know why. Either you were blocking on the receiving end (with some unconscious thought you were not aware of), or you had too much fear of receiving what you asked for. Or perhaps what you asked for was not really good for you, and your higher self knew it.

Let's say you asked for something, but you had too much fear of receiving it. What you need to know is that the Holy Spirit will never add to your fear; and therefore, it would not be good for you to have what you asked for until you worked out your fear. A Course in Miracles would explain it this way: Let's say you are praying for an overnight cure for a certain disease. However, a sudden miracle may be such a threat to your thought system that you cannot allow this to happen for yourself.

What you need to do first is pray for a release of the fear of having the miracle. Ultimately pray for help in the resolution of the cause of your fear (which would be the belief in the separation). When prayers are not answered, do not blame God. Only you can deprive yourself of anything. The Source is abundant and wants to give to you. The giver expands by giving. God wants you to have all the gifts of the Kingdom.

The initial phase of prayer is one of emptying. Pouring out the contents of your heart (emptying the cup) without editing or embarrassment. Withholding nothing is a prerequisite to attain perfection in prayer. In the privacy of one's inner sanctum, a complete housecleaning of all afflicting emotions must be achieved before there is room for God's grace. (What I do is write a letter to God or my guru to express all my stuff.)

One of the methods of prayer I learned as a child is very effective. It contains five parts.

1. Opening
2. Forgiveness
3. Gratitude
4. Petition
5. Closing

l. Opening: This is for setting the stage, creating the ambiance, establishing the connection. Read from the scriptures or from a spiritual book. What we do is open the text of ACIM and read a few paragraphs or pages.

2. Forgiveness: This when you ask for pardon for anything you feel is your wrongdoing. You also ask to be forgiven by any specific person. Or you forgive someone you need to forgive.

3. Gratitude: This is where you specifically express gratitude for the things you have: friends, love, the life you have, your health, etc. Remember whatever you are grateful for increases.

4. Petition: Now you are in the proper context to ask for help or guidance in any specific area. Talk to the Holy Spirit freely, knowing that by having faith you will receive the help.

5. Closing: This is again, when you read spiritual literature. It would be a good time to read ACIM lesson for the day.

This prayer technique can be done alone or with your mate, whole family, or friends. It is very good to do it out loud with others. I have given this simple prayer technique to couples on the verge of divorce and they told me it saved their marriage.

Of course, asking and begging are lower forms of prayer. The highest form of prayer is gratitude and your celebration of your connection to the Source. I refer you to ACIM sequel called *The Song of Prayer.* I will paraphrase a few paragraphs here.

Prayer is practice of the presence of God. A thankful mind attracts good. Try to get to the point where you are then giving thanks instead of complaining, fearing, or worrying.

If you do petition, pray from the standpoint of already having what you ask for.

Knowing there is no spiritual lack, give thanks then, that it is already done.

1. *Lay hold of the good you desire*
2. *Recognize it is here and now*
3. *Have absolute confidence*
4. *Express gratitude*

Ask, and believing, you shall receive. Faith is everything. When you develop a consciousness of the things you seek, they will appear in your presence.

God meets you at the level of your consciousness. If your consciousness of need is greater than your consciousness of God, then the need will expand.

When you love God more than your problem, you will be healed, and your prayers will be answered.

God can work through you only when your consciousness and His are one. When you are conscious of your oneness with God, then you can embody Him. Prayer does help clear the way for your acceptance of the oneness, yes, and yet the more you accept the oneness before prayer, the better will be your response.

Affirmations are also like prayers that you impress onto Infinite Spirit to create a desired result. Always thinking in affirmations will keep you in a constant state of prayer.

I find it very effective to talk out loud to God when I am praying. I usually write letters to my guru which are prayers, but I tend to talk to Jesus out loud. I don't know why, but it always works. This can feel embarrassing at first; however, try it. It helps you stay conscious, and it is a very deep experience. Do this in the woods or at night in your bedroom by yourself.

#6.

AN AISLE FOR ENLIGHTENED BOOKS

All people need enlightened books to read. We have well stocked shelves in aisle six. Why not make a pact with yourself to read only enlightened books for a while?

By this I mean, why not read only books where the author understands that thoughts create results? (Otherwise, a whole book could lead to confusion.) These books not only are spiritually uplifting they are also able to accelerate your process and help you stay high.

Naturally, we hope you will be inspired to read the books we have written. They are listed here, with short synopsis of each and the link where you can purchase them: *bit.ly/BooksRay*. What if you took a whole year to read nothing but enlightened books? Everyone who has actually done this has thanked us profusely for the recommendation.

The first book I am going to single out here is A Course in Miracles. It was published in 1976, and I was aware of it a little bit before that. Before it came out, one of my friends sent me a photo-copied chapter and wrote in big red letters with a magic marker on the front, "Sondra, Read This Immediately!" Well, I did, and I could not believe what I was reading. It was a direct hit of enlightenment coming into my crown chakra!

#1. A Course in Miracles by Jesus, the Christ

What would you do if you knew there was someone who knew all the answers to all problems; someone who had mastered life completely, someone who could put you into instant joy, someone who could heal you, someone who had even conquered death? Would you read a book by that person?

What would you do if you knew Jesus was still around and you could find Him? Would you check Him out, even if you were not raised a Christian? I hope you would. What would you do if you knew there was a book downloaded by Him in the last few decades, a book given by Him for modern times? A book that cleared up all the confusion in the Bible, and all the confusion you might have had in religion; a book that explained everything, answered all questions and taught you how to heal yourself completely? And what if this book taught you how to have perfect relationships? What if this book itself was a miracle? Would you read it? You might at least consider it, right?

That book is here! Jesus is here through it. The answers are in it. That book is A Course in Miracles. Perhaps you have heard about it, but have you actually studied it? You can have the answers now. You can be healed now. You can receive salvation now. Your life can work now.

I think this book is the most important book written in 2,000 years! Seriously! Personally, I feel it is important to learn from someone who has mastered what we are trying to learn. The problem with learning from someone like Jesus is that one has to confront their old feelings about the subject of Jesus and religion. This is, however, Jesus for modern times.

Do you know that the foundation of Christianity was actually written down about 30 years after Jesus' death and resurrection, and much of it was written in a way that can easily be misinterpreted? Since it was written by those who had not necessarily cleared their egos completely, there were mistakes. The ego is based on the thought that one is separate from God. It would be possible for anyone who had that thought to write something rather deceptive, even though they had good intentions.

Maybe it is time to re-examine all of our religious conditioning. And that is what A Course in Miracles does: it is a correction of religion. The Course is not a religion; it is a correction. One of my teachers of ACIM said that when Jesus was on the planet, He was so pure and that He purged so much ego, that it has taken 2,000 years to process it. Now, after all this time, we are ready to hear the next set of words from Him.

ACIM is really the second coming. Now He is saying that we did not understand before; we are getting another chance. All we have to do is to have the willingness to read it and really follow it this time.

Why would someone not read it? Maybe they are on a different path and that is fine. But maybe you are one of those who have never heard of it. If so, I am honored to be the one to tell you about it. But what if *it is* for you and you are just resisting it? Then ask yourself these questions:

Am I afraid of having it all, and feeling good?
Am I choosing pain over joy?
Am I too addicted to my negativity to recognize a good thing like this?
Am I angry at God and fed up with anything with a religious tone?
Am I being stubborn and rebellious and loving my misery?

If you answer yes to any of these questions, you may have convinced yourself you do not need the Course and/or should not read it. Are you willing to see it differently?

As I told you, the way I found A Course in Miracles before it was officially published was when a friend sent me the first chapter of the text and wrote in red on the first page: "Sondra, read this immediately!" Who does that? Have you ever had a friend send you something like that? I am so grateful to him because when I read the chapter he sent, I then ran out and got the books ASAP. If he had not done that, I may have delayed. By then they were published in a three-volume set: Text, Workbook, Teacher's Manual.

- ❖ If you have never bought the book, I hope you will buy it. (Also free on line: www.miraclecenter.org/a-course-in-miracles/)
- ❖ If you have bought it and have not opened it, I ask you to open it.
- ❖ If you have opened it and quit on a certain lesson, I hope you will go back and start again on that lesson.
- ❖ If you have trouble getting started, at least put the book in your bed and sleep with it so you get the high frequency. It is all Christ Consciousness. Maybe one day you will roll over and open it.

You start with the lessons and read one lesson a day for 365 days. Do not begin with the Text without also starting the Workbook, because the Text is too deep. The Workbook is written in practical, simple language that helps you understand the Text. If you get the One Volume ACIM, the Text is in the beginning of the book because that came down first. Read 10 lessons over 10 days in the Workbook, and then go and read one chapter in the text while you are doing the ten lessons. To help you understand the Text, I wrote a book called *Drinking the Divine*, and I outlined it all.

There may be tremendous resistance to sticking with it at first. That is just your ego. Go beyond it. As your ego starts to dissolve, you will begin to see how the Course makes so much sense. I went through that. Then on the third round of reading it, I actually said, "This is the only thing that makes sense to me." Here is an example of a paragraph from the text:

> *No right mind can believe that its will is stronger than God's. If, then, a mind believes that its will is different from Him, it can only decide either that there is no God or that God's will is fearful. The former accounts for the atheist and the latter for the martyr, who believes that God demands sacrifice. Either of these insane decisions will induce panic, because the atheist believes he is alone, and the martyr that God is crucifying him. (ACIM; Text; Chap. 9; Sec. I; ¶8)*

The logic of ACIM makes things clear, but sometimes a second and third reading is required in order for the truth to sink into our consciousness. We can get it, but like all deep wisdom, it requires our commitment and attention.

You will definitely climb the ladder of your holiness working with the principles laid out in A Course in Miracles. Bringing the principles into application in your life is a very meaningful thing to do. In *The Supermarket for a Meaningful Life*, I would say when it comes to enlightened books, ACIM is on the top of my book list.

#2. *Leaves of Grass* by Walt Whitman

This is Markus. The most powerful invocation I ever read/heard was written by Walt Whitman over 150 years ago. The opening to the poem, "Leaves of Grass" starts like this:

> *I celebrate myself,*
> *And what I assume you shall assume,*
> *For every atom belonging to me as good belongs to you.*
>
> *I loafe and invite my soul,*
> *I lean and loafe at my ease.... observing a spear of*
> *summer grass.*

Just six short lines contain the whole of Western egalitarian thought. They contain the appeal to Higher Truth. And they contain the actual inclusion of the natural elements that make us up in this celebration of our physical and spiritual existence.

The artist is an observer more than he is a participant in the dramas of life. He has participated, yes. But when it comes time for his artistic expression, he is a witness who translates what he has seen through the medium he has mastered. In Whitman's case, words—poetical strings of words, direct and poignant—paint a vivid picture of the world he sees. As an observer of life, he can also be a "loafer." The word takes on a new meaning—relaxed, ready, free, acutely aware, non-judgmental, in a state of divine leisure, applied to the present moment. I want to join him there on the grass, observing, sharing the "atoms belonging to him," that belong to me also.

With poetry, or any profound writing or speaking, we have to listen more attentively in order to glean the meaning of what is being transmitted. Naturally, we would. Attention brings us depth and understanding. Also, we need to start with the premise, "I don't know," and if the author is worth reading at all, he or she will be communicating from that vast reservoir of the unknown. What he writes will be a revelation not only to his readers, but most likely to himself as well of the very thing he is communicating.

> Afoot and light-hearted I take to the open road,
> Healthy, free, the world before me,
> The long brown path before me leading wherever I choose.
>
> Henceforth I ask not good-fortune, I myself am good-fortune,
> Henceforth I whimper no more, postpone no more, need nothing,
> Done with indoor complaints, libraries, querulous criticisms,
> Strong and content I travel the open road.

This passage is from "Song of the Open Road." It gives us the world of freedom, adventure, infinite possibilities. "I ask not good-fortune, I myself am good-fortune." This is a statement of total self-esteem, total self-confidence, total liberation from the confines of indoor "complaints and criticisms." Even if one finds himself in these indoor confinements during this great sequester, a few moments spent with Whitman can get you out of doors into the spiritual realms of a world free of all inhibitions. A few lines of Whitman can take you beyond even your own self-imposed thoughts of limitation.

> I myself am good-fortune.

Could we live like this? There would be no need to ever doubt ourselves again. There would be no fear of the future—what will life provide for me into perpetuity? Life is not so much asked to provide because I have my own resources within myself—I myself am good-fortune.

Whitman was a motivational speaker 150 years before there was such a thing. He wrote words that broke the mold. And he wrote them in a way a person with an average education could grok and glean something from them if they took just a little time to listen.

He takes us into the very heart of poetic inquiry in "Song of Myself":

> *Have you reckon'd a thousand acres much? Have you*
> *   reckon'd the earth much?*
> *Have you practis'd so long to learn to read?*
> *Have you felt so proud to get the meaning of poems?*
>
> *Stop this day and night with me and you shall possess the*
> *   origin of all poems,*
> *You shall possess the good of the earth and sun, (there are*
> *   millions of suns left,)*
> *You shall no longer take things at second hand or third hand,*
> *   nor look through the eyes of the dead, nor feed on the*
> *   spectres in books,*
> *You shall not look through my eyes either, nor take things*
> *   from me,*
> *You shall listen to all sides and filter them from yourself.*

Whitman is the quintessential poet. If one had never read poetry before, the new depth of one's soul can be awakened by reading one short or long poem by Walt Whitman. You can feel that "ah-ha" from the inspiration gained from this kind of reading. You can begin to possess the "origin of all poems" by reading Whitman. You will get a first-hand experience of things. And this will not be the opinions of the writer, but the discoveries made within yourself, in your own encounter with a life immortal.

Reading Whitman takes you into a treasure trove of insights into your soul that you may not find anywhere else. He speaks to you. The gap between his heart and yours is diminished so much that you very well may beat a pulse in tandem with his by the time you are finished reading. You will not be the same afterward. And this is the litmus test of spiritually uplifting books—you are transformed for the better. Whitman guarantees this.

3. *Divine Lessons from Amma* by Amritanadamayi

Holy Mother Amritanandamayi is esteemed as a stupendous incarnation of the Divine Mother herself. Today she is India's leading female light. She selflessly travels the world to console, hug, heal, and inspire her millions of children with the power of divine love. We are some of her fortunate children and we have no proper words to express the inner joy when we just think of her. She takes into her lap thousands and thousands of people every day; all ages, religious races, and walks of life. She absorbs their suffering and negativity into her own body and transmutes it to nil. She blesses us all and heals us all with her gentle caress. She was even known to hug 20,000 people in one day! It has been said that "the lady of love, simply known as *AMMA*, may be the greatest phenomenon in the history of religion." We agree that she certainly has emerged as one of the most powerful spiritual masters ever to walk the planet. Her body vibrates with tremendous power (shakti) of divine love. It is as though she is connected to an electrical current that supercharges her biological structure. Go to her website www.Amma.org and see when her schedule will take her near you. You can order her books there as well.

I have ordered all her books. I love to read her words and stories. I underline what strikes me and then I go back and back and reread those lines over again.

Here are some of her statements that are profound:

> A true disciple is one who is willing to surrender everything to God or the Guru and desires nothing but the attainment of Supreme Knowledge. He wants to be disciplined by the Master. Whatever

may come, a real disciple will not leave the Master until he attains the Supreme State. For him everything is the Guru. Strongly bound to the Guru in his total surrender, he has no other choice but to seek the Guru's grace. Fully aware that Perfection cannot be attained without the Guru's grace, he knows that he needs to empty his mind in order to receive it. The Guru or God is his beloved. For him every word or deed is a prayer, a worship of his Beloved. He is always in a blissful mood as a result. (pp. 111-113 from Awaken Children Volume IV)

The guru is like the sun. He just shines. He cannot do otherwise. He just shines and whoever keeps the doors of his heart open receives the light God simply is. He has no conditions and no limits. If the door of your heart is closed, He will not come in. He is not aggressive because He is love. He will wait outside but He will not break in. Love is not aggressive. Love is a constant uninterrupted and unbreakable flow. The Guru is not an ego. He is the Universe. He can accommodate anything and everything. He is extraordinary. He is ordinary too. Whatever you say about Him will be wrong because the Guru cannot be explained. He cannot be reduced to words. (p. 201 from Awaken Children Volume IV)

The guru is like a magnet. There are three types of people. Very few are like steel, which becomes magnetized just by being close to the magnet. Even when the original magnet is removed, the steel does not lose its magnetic power but retains it. Such is the first-rate disciple. Such disciples will later become Gurus themselves. The second group of people is like raw iron; it gets drawn by the magnet. However, once the magnet is removed, the raw iron will lose its magnetic power. Most of us feel extremely drawn to the Mahatma, but the moment we will move away, we will go back to pursuing material pleasures and selfish interests. Most people belong to the third category. Such people are like pieces of wood. Even being placed right before the magnet (that is the Mahatma) will make no difference. Such people are not even drawn to the Mahatma. (pp.149 & 150 from Unforgettable Memories)

Questioner: Amma, what is your definition of unconditional love and compassion?
Amma: It is a totally undefinable state.
Questioner: Then, what is it?
Amma: It is expansiveness like the sky.
Questioner: Is it the inner sky?
Amma: There is no inside and outside there.
Questioner: Then?
Amma: There is only oneness. That is why it cannot be defined.
(p. 129 From Amma's Heart)

Try not to create any difficulties or suffering for others. The easy way is to make every action an offering to the Supreme Being. Think of every action as a form of worship. Then our actions will make both us and others happy and will benefit us and others as well. From now on, try to imagine that everyone who comes to you has been sent to you by God. If you can do this, you will surely change. By forming our actions as worship to God, not only we, but society as a whole will benefit. Our lives will become relatively peaceful and harmonious if we know what our attitude should be when we perform our actions and enjoy their fruits. (pp. 125 & 126 from Lead Us to Purity)

Think of the frenzy if you were trying to escape from fire. You have to cry with that same urgency to get the vision of God. Think of how someone who falls into deep water and cannot swim would struggle for breath. That's how much you have to struggle to merge in the Supreme Absolute. You should constantly feel the grief of not having attained the vision of God. At every moment, your heart should ache for it. You need to feel, "I don't want anything but God." You should truly love God. Without love, no amount of Japa and meditation will bear fruit. When your love for God becomes very strong, all the bad vasanas within you will automatically drop away. Love for God is like a sail that helps the boat go forward. A real sadhak (spiritual seeker) doesn't like anything that isn't related to God. Living with the thought of God always in his mind, he can't bear any obstacles that come between himself and God. Compared to his love for God, everything else is worthless to him. (pp. 41 & 134 from Eternal Wisdom)

The true teacher of life, the "Satguru" as they are called in India, is a wellspring of wisdom that never runs dry. The words of a true teacher will be true in whatever age they are uttered. Reading their words is like taking a spiritual bath in the timeless wisdom of the ages.

4. *How to Raise a Child of God* by Tara Singh

This is Markus. I had the great privilege of knowing Tara Singh and receiving his wisdom directly for 17 years, from 1989 to 2006 when he made his transition. Words can hardly describe my *life-for-life* relationship with him. To say he took me to places I could not have gone on my own is an understatement. I wrote the best I could of my time with him in my first book, *Miracles with My Master, Tara Singh.* (bit.ly/TSRay)

Of all the books Tara Singh scribed (and all of them are worthy of reading and studying closely) I would have to say *How to Raise a Child of God* is a book for parents and also people who are not parents. It fulfills a need in us that was not fulfilled in our youth. We were channeled and pushed, directed and led into systems of education that promoted the learning of skills for the most part. The deeper freedoms and purpose of life were not so well addressed, and we ended up being conditioned human beings. We were programmed to a degree to fit in to the familial, religious, economic, and social systems. These skills were needed, of course, but there was a greater part of our awakening totally overlooked.

Tara Singh addresses this need in *How to Raise a Child of God.*

> *The function of education is to awaken man to the Call to Wisdom and Freedom and to his own God-created, eternal Self. Instead, by imparting skills and not Knowledge, education has served only as a means of survival. It enslaves man to the body and the brain; it does not introduce him to his free spirit. It bolsters a culture of*

irresponsibility and promotes not life, but death. Education is to awaken you to who you are; then you will know all there is. The Mind of man, lit with the light of heaven, can have no sense of lack. It sees only what God created. (p. 41 from How to Raise a Child of God)

Perhaps this is a hard pill to swallow. Yet, who has answered this call to wisdom and freedom Tara Singh speaks about as the true function of education? You who are reading this book must have some sense of it, or you would not have gotten this far.

Have we lost our ability to question? Or are we conditioned by our routines for survival? The wise would question our motives at all levels of life and ask us why we are doing that. Are we doing what we are doing for merely the body's survival? pleasure? sense of status? pride? greed? fear? Are we outgrowing things for the evolution of our souls? What does it mean to awaken ourselves?

There are some people who are highly evolved. How do we know that? Because their process of outgrowing is very rapid. What would take a normal person fifty years to outgrow, they outgrow in ten. For most people, during fifty years they become more entrenched, more involved. Thus, it takes a longer time to undo and to outgrow. What this process of postponement has done to the personality! Finally, when they come to urgency, they see how much burden they carry—their mental attics and cellars are crowded and need to be cleansed. Great people do not accumulate; they can quickly see the essence, the fact, the principle, the law, and outgrow. (p. 91 from How to Raise a Child of God)

The introduction of this book is filled with the story of Tara Singh's education in life. Coming from an affluent Sikh family, he was not so inclined toward conventional schooling. His learning was more from the encounters with wise people he met along the way. His friends were the likes of Prime Minister Nehru, Mrs. Eleanor Roosevelt, Supreme Court Justice William O. Douglass. His teachers included the teacher of the Dalai Lama, Mr. J Krishnamurti, and Dr. Helen Schucman, the scribe of A Course in Miracles. He was able to meet and glean the wisdom from these great souls. It was an education of the highest order, free and aspiring to the basic questions of life—its purpose and process, its depth and meaning, its demands and responsibilities.

> *We think and we teach the child to think. Thought is of the earth; its roots are of fear and survival. What would it be if our thoughts were Thoughts of God? Would the child not learn that? He need never know relative knowledge—"this" versus "that." If the parents, having understood this, attempt to greet the child with thought that has no duality in it, then the Force that protects the child's Divine Leisure would be assisting them as well. They will have called upon It. That same Divine Force that assures the child's needs are met, is at their disposal too, if they become receptive. (p. 124 from How to Raise a Child of God)*

As you can see this is a different type of education. It incorporates the connection to Divine Forces into the regular workings of everyday life—not in a fanatical way, but in a natural inclusion of the sacredness of being into all that we do. But we must be attentive to it. We must call upon it to actually be in our awareness. Without this invocation we will most likely fall into the conditioning so prevalent in our modern world of algorithms and market manipulations.

I will end this summary with these passages about discipline:

> *What we commonly call discipline is not discipline at all. Generation after generation we have clipped the very wings of the child, taking away his vulnerability, taking away his spontaneity by putting on him a mold that is made of time and not space. That is the discipline that we know. It is very important that we get to know it thoroughly. Could you come*

to a place in you that is not prejudiced and conditioned? By doing so you would make more space within yourself just by seeing how wrong it is and how it has damaged, molded, and confined you....

....See how the conditioning has limited you, made you a citizen rather than a human being. You would begin to touch upon a space within you that is incorruptible. And that is what you would want to impart to your child rather than external conformity. Then your disciplining of the child would awaken him not to be false. If you don't have the space, then you impose. If you have the space, you awaken. The real meaning of the word discipline is to awaken. (p. 269 from How to Raise a Child of God)

5. *Physical Immortality* by Sondra Ray

This is Markus. I refer to one of our own books here because I think it is of paramount importance for every human being on the planet to understand how life works, which means also to understand how death works. *Physical Immortality: How to Overcome Death* is the book Sondra and I wrote on this topic, mostly a revision of a former book she wrote on the same subject. This conversation is important so people can have a clear comprehension of why they are responsible for their own death (even if it seems like it just happens to people). "Death" as we know it, the cessation of the body's functioning, is caused by consciousness. And it is important to look at the part of consciousness that attracts the factors and conditions in the mind and body which result in death.

Basically, everyone has what we call an *unconscious death urge*. It is composed of three major components:

1. The belief that death is inevitable
2. The most negative thought you hold about yourself
3. Your imagined separation from your Source of Life

There are other factors as well composing the unconscious death urge, but these are the main ones. Others include loyalty to family patterns and diseases that brought about death; self-destructive lifestyles; depression; lack of energy for your life purpose; accumulations of non-forgiveness; anger and resentment; and your secret wish to die if you hate your life. Everyone has an unconscious death urge that they will have to deal with sooner or later, even if it is in future lifetimes. Unless your parents were both immortal yogis, you were "programmed" to die at a certain age. So how do we un-program ourselves and live as long as we choose? This is the subject of this book.

Physical Immortality questions the whole complex of human conditioning around death. It is one of the most important books you could ever read in this lifetime. It could free you from your unconscious death urge and put immortal life back into your awareness of your Divine Power and Destiny. It could extend your life beyond belief and give you a real sacred mission that transcends mere survival. Would you want that? If you notice yourself saying no for various reasons, those reasons are part of your unconscious death urge.

Sondra tells us why she wrote on such a controversial topic:

> I wrote this book because I am a healer and I wanted to help people not only heal themselves but prevent sickness. Once I came to understand that the "unconscious death urge" is one of the main causes of sickness, I felt an obligation to write about this. We could teach people how to heal anything, but if we don't teach them how death works, they will heal—perhaps; but they will just make up a new way to kill themselves. People have to understand that all death is suicide and people kill themselves with their own thoughts. Especially with their submerged, subconscious thoughts.
>
> Another reason this book was important to write was because people have a lot of fear. Fear makes one weak, and it is no fun. Besides, what you fear you attract. I came to understand that death is the stronghold of all fear. If people can clear out their own

death urge through Liberation Breathing, for example, their fear will dissolve. Whenever you feel fear in any form (and you are fearful if you don't feel deep contentment) be sure you have made an idol leading to death. (page xxv from Physical Immortality)

She mentions Liberation Breathing as a way to clear ourselves of our unconscious death urge. We have found that breathwork in general, Liberation Breathing in particular (which is our form of breathwork from the Divine Mother), is the most effective way to clear out our memories of dying that are held in our subconscious mind. All thoughts of limitation and memories of trauma contribute greatly to our death, so we have to have a way of clearing them from our mind, but also from the cellular memory of the body. Liberation Breathing does this quicker than any other yoga, therapy, or breathing meditation. The point of any spiritual clearing is to help us to overcome death, in mind and body.

People have a hard time thinking life in the body can be immortal, or a function of immortal thoughts of God. They have a better time believing that the spirit is immortal, but life in the body is an illusion subject to a different set of laws of time and dissolution. But these are still beliefs that can be questioned and changed. The Bible speaks of characters who lived hundreds of years in a kind of constant holy communion. How did they do it? They certainly did not do it thinking life in the body will terminate after eighty years, or a hundred years. They certainly did not do it believing that entropic forces make the body wear out eventually for good. How did they overcome a premature death?

Let me close this section with the following quotation from Ann and Peter Meyer's book, Being a Christ:

It helps to remember also that Spirit, Mind and Body are really the same substance but have different activities at different vibrations, just like steam, water and ice are the same element but have different properties at different temperatures. (p. 64)

A yogi once told me this: "Spirit is that which cannot be destroyed. Mind is condensed spirit. Body is condensed mind. Therefore, body is utmost spirit." Knowing that, Physical Immortality makes sense.

An ice cube is solid water; heat it up and it is liquid; heat it up more and it becomes invisible as steam. Perhaps this is how Immortal Masters like Babaji and Jesus can dematerialize their bodies. They increase the frequency of their physical cells to become invisible. (p. 62 from Physical Immortality)

Okay, this is far-out thinking and stretches your mind. But why not stretch your mind? This is not just California New Age jargon from the '70s and '80s. This is a relevant subject during this great sequester to think about. What is the purpose for Life if the grim reaper is going to take it from us against our will? Would it not be more prudent to use this time to unravel our own unconscious death urge and take responsibility for our life or our death?

Until we clear our unconscious death urge, we will not have constant joy, and this is the purpose of Life: to be in a state of perfect happiness that is so strong that it extends our life indefinitely, into perpetuity. In order to do this, we have to reverse the three main causes of death:

1. We have to change all negative thoughts we hold about ourselves by seeing that they are not absolutely true (therefore they are lies that do not actually exist apart from our projecting them onto life).
2. We have to give up the thought "death is inevitable" and see that life and death, as well as health of the body or sickness of the body, are functions of consciousness. We have to change all thoughts that are literally programming us to die.
3. We have to nurture and develop a Divine Connection to our Source Energy, in which we are certain of this supernatural Spiritual Life Force that created us and maintains us. We need

to develop an intense gratitude for this benevolent Life Force that does not put a shelf life on our bodies.

If we are willing to do these things, we may have a different view of life in this great sequester, and after this great sequester.

These five books could change your life. These five books would fulfill your deepest yearnings for wisdom. They are an answer to your call. Socrates and other great beings of the spirit said, "Know Thyself." These five books will get you going on an adventure of Self-discovery the likes of which you probably have never gone. This list is not exhaustive. There is much great wisdom out there. These are our top choices. Don't delay in starting your own library of great wisdom and conversations with the wise. The Aisle for Enlightened Books is by far one of the most important, in *The Supermarket for a Meaningful Life.*

#7.

AN AISLE FOR SPIRITUAL MASTERS

People need a spiritual master. These masters give their wisdom in aisle seven. At a time like this when everything is in chaos it is extremely helpful to have a spiritual master. It really helps to keep you from going crazy. Some people mistakenly think that if you have a guru or a master, then you have to give your power away. In my experience nothing could be farther from the truth. My experience is that a true master helps you get into your own power and stand on your own feet; and this happens as fast as you can take it. In the presence of a master, we are able to touch our own wholeness and our own perfection faster. As you get closer to the master, you find more and more of your true self.

The guru is a mirror. Only in this case, you see yourself magnified a lot and you have to face yourself like never before. This is good because you can let go of junk sooner and this is always better for you.

For me it was a deep, deep, yearning for the truth, a deep longing to know perfect love, a desire to know all that life could be, a craving for divinity—and that is what drew me to be a seeker. My master Babaji responded to this yearning and longing in my heart, helped me dispel my ignorance, my limitations, my fears, my karma, my ego, and all that kept me from knowing my own inner divine nature. I could not resist his outpouring of Divine Love. Why should I, when it is there for the asking? I asked and I was answered.

Markus and I have three main masters: Babaji, Jesus of A Course in Miracles, and the Divine Mother. We call them the DREAM TEAM. You can have them available to you also. Babaji always said, "My love is available. You can take it or not." I always say, "Why not?" We need all the help we can get.

WHO IS BABAJI?

Babaji, also named Sri Sri 1008 Bhagwan Herakhan Wale Baba, is an immortal maha avatar and yogi master. Avatar means "descent of the Divine into matter." That means He manifested his body from the light, like Melchizedek in the Bible, who "had no father, nor mother" in Hebrews. So Babaji is an emanation of Divine Light, Who, out of compassion, manifested in human form on earth to urge humanity to progress on the path of truth, love, simplicity, and service to mankind. That was His formula for happiness. He is the power of the Eternal Father, Mother, and Divine Child. He can assume any form He wishes and can change that form at any time. I have seen Him bi-locate. In fulfillment of ancient scriptural and prophetic predictions, He materialized a youthful body in 1970, in a cave near the village of Haidakhan in the foothills of the Himalayas. (Yogananda wrote about Him in the book *Autobiography of a Yogi*; Chapters 33 & 34) Indian devotees tell stories of seeing a ball of light in the cave. And when He came out, He climbed to the top of Mt. Kailash above the cave and sat there 45 days and nights without eating, drinking, or sleeping. His energy was so strong that He had to keep his eyes shut all those days or else people would faint in His presence. Indian people who were there told me that they would have constant visions of their past lives and future lives in His presence.

Babaji was accessible for 14 years on that last visit. And yet, He has not ever really left, because He does not come and go. He was and is omnipresent. He is the greatest manifestation of divine joy in human form. He is Divine Joy itself. His form is limitless and beyond scope of time. He is the essence of all religions and transcends every belief. He teaches through vibrations and direct experience in a way that words cannot express. To try to explain Him on paper is totally inadequate. To be with Him or experience Him answers all questions.

It is my humblest desire to make it known to you that any story I relate to you about Babaji is given with the intention to let you know that He is just as available to you and for all as He is to Markus and me. In fact, just yesterday He appeared to one of our clients during her Liberation Breathing session and totally cleared her out. She has never been to India, but she is tapped in and willing to receive His help. Markus has been to India with me many times but did not meet Babaji personally in this life. He was with Him in other lives, and he has surrendered to Babaji and receives transmissions from Him very frequently. He wrote many poems to Him in our book, *Babaji, My Miraculous Meetings with a Maha Avatar.* (bit.ly/BabajiRay)

There is a ceremonial prayer called the Aarti, which is sung to Babaji in Sanskrit. One of the lines we love the most from it is this: "Thou art a never-failing spring of bliss." That is and always has been our experience of Babaji, who has been with us on Earth in human form countless times since life began. Jesus is said to have visited Babaji in Benares during His travels and studies in the East. It was there that Babaji shaved Jesus's head and blessed Him before he started his ministry. There are actual books that relate that. In many sacred texts it was written that when righteousness declines, God creates for Himself a body and comes to live on Earth. He appears and makes Himself known to those who seek Him. In the Bhagavad-Gita 4:8, it reads as follows:

> When righteousness is weak and the wicked and unrighteousness exult in pride, then my Spirit arises on Earth. For the salvation of those who are good, for the destruction of evil in men, for the fulfillment of the kingdom of righteousness, I come to this world in the ages that pass.

The Gospel of St. Thomas says:

> If you see Him who has not been born of a woman, throw your face to the ground and worship Him—He is your Father.

Babaji taught that through the practice of karma yoga (work dedicated to divine service of God) man purifies and protects himself. "Work is worship" is a statement He often made. He taught a philosophy of action. He would often say, "An idle man is a dead man."

While He was physically present with us, and while He would be standing right there, He would also be busy all over the world at the same time. The glory of Him is greater than the mind could grasp. At times when He walked, He left no footprints. He would run up a hill as though wings were attached to his feet.

To show you that He is the *real deal,* check this out: From time-to-time certain symbols appeared on the soles of His feet which are known in the Indian spiritual traditions as cosmic marks:

❖ The Sanskrit letter OM
❖ The Shesh Nag (five hooded snake symbolizing the five senses)
❖ Conch shells
❖ A trident
❖ Head of a bull
❖ Swastick (symbol of peace and success)
❖ A peacock
❖ A lotus flower
❖ A bow
❖ A chakra
❖ The crescent moon
❖ All signs of the zodiac
❖ The serpent
❖ The sun
❖ An octagon
❖ A hatchet
❖ An eagle
❖ The planetary system

These marks fulfill the predictions delivered long ago that when Shiva was next to appear in human form, He would have these symbols.

His spiritual significance has always been beyond comprehension. "Shiva" means eternally joyous and auspicious, the God without second Who has been moving in this world in His form since creation. He is described as ever pure, changeless, all pervading, eternal, the immortal essence of the universe, the universal Self, the self-resplendent light of lights, the embodiment of wisdom, capable of doing anything at any moment, of whatever magnitude. I can tell you this: The guru's love will intoxicate you.

Now you see why they call Him the guru of gurus. Although He said very little and mostly worked on energy vibrations, here is one of His speeches that is magnificent:

> *Love and serve all humanity.*
> *Assist everyone.*
> *Be cheerful. Be courteous.*
> *Be a dynamo of irrepressible happiness.*
> *See God and good in every face.*
> *There is no saint without a past;*
> *There is no sinner without a future.*
> *Praise every soul;*
> *If you cannot praise someone—then*
> *Let them pass out of your life.*
> *Be original. Be inventive.*
> *Dare, dare and then dare more.*
> *Do not imitate. Stand on your own ground.*
> *Do not lean on the borrowed staff of others.*
> *Think your own thoughts.*
> *Be yourself.*
> *All perfection and all virtues of the*
> *Deity are hidden inside you. Reveal them.*
> *The savior, also, is already within you.*
> *Reveal Him. Let His grace emancipate you.*
> *Let your life be that of a rose: though silent,*
> *It speaks in the language of fragrance.*

We have written two whole books on Babaji. One I mentioned above is *Babaji: My Miraculous Meetings with a Maha Avatar.* This is a major work with many photos and paintings of Babaji that Markus painted, as well as his poems to Babaji. The other small book we wrote is *The Perfection of Babaji* (bit.ly/PerfectionRay) This includes all my direct visions of Him and teachings He gave me after he took Samadhi (conscious departure from His body).

JESUS OF A COURSE IN MIRACLES

Markus on ACIM

In the late 1960s an unprecedented event took place in America. The second coming of Jesus, the Christ, was in full force. And hardly anyone knew it was happening. It took place amidst the most unexpected circumstances.

Dr. Helen Schucman, a professor at Columbia University in New York, began to receive dictation from a Voice; and that Voice was from none other than Jesus Himself. His *second coming* was upon the human race, and this time He did not even need a body to do it. He sent His mind! That was all that was needed. He sent His mind, and the remarkable abilities of this lady, a clinical psychologist and educator were there to receive it. She was there to diligently record His mind for all of mankind. Such a feat had never taken place quite in this way. An enlightened being, the Christ, had just given the human race a roadmap for their own spiritual awakening. Not only a roadmap, but an actual course in miracles. A scripture had not ever been given in this way by an enlightened being, which so thoroughly and methodically provides a doorway into the dimension of the Heaven state of being—to the higher and true self that God created. Quietly stunned, Dr. Schucman accepted her destiny: She was the "mother of Jesus's mind."

The Course was dictated to her between the years of 1965 to 1972. The writing was never automatic. Her inner dialogue with Him could be started or stopped at any time. A Course in Miracles was published in

1976 and has been disseminated around the world ever since in many different languages. One could understand its purpose and practice in this short introduction:

> *This is a course in miracles. It is a required course. Only the time you take it is voluntary. Free will does not mean that you can establish the curriculum. It means only that you can elect what you want to take at a given time. The course does not aim at teaching the meaning of love, for that is beyond what can be taught. It does aim, however, at removing the blocks to the awareness of love's presence, which is your natural inheritance. The opposite of love is fear, but what is all-encompassing can have no opposite. This course can therefore be summed up very simply in this way:*
>
> *Nothing real can be threatened.*
> *Nothing unreal exits.*
> *Herein lies the peace of God*

We have to read it differently. We have to allow the words to go in and ask for the state of mind beyond the words to be made manifest in us. In other words, application is more important than learning and understanding. We are asking the Higher Forces to make this application possible in us. We are asking to be filled with the Spirit of Truth. We are asking for the Christ to be made manifest in us. This is the true communion: we are asking Christ's Mind to enter in and transform our own mind. Jesus says in the text, "This is a course in mind training."

What would bring the *second coming* to us?

1. First, accepting the fact that A Course in Miracles is Jesus's message given to us in these times directly.
2. Then, seeing that He is attempting to enter our mind to re-train it, start with practicing the principles laid out in the Workbook and Text of A Course in Miracles.

The second coming is Jesus coming to you. Who else would he be coming to? You! You are the one He is trying to reach. You are the one from whom He is attempting to "remove the blocks to the awareness of love's presence." You are the one to whom He is trying to give "your natural inheritance" of Self-identity. You are the one He wants to free from the conflict of opposites and the fears of survival. You are the one upon whom He wishes to bestow the stillness of the peace of God.

The time we take to wake up is entirely up to us. We have the free will to accept it, reject, or delay in our decision. A spiritual master like Jesus comes to us directly through A Course in Miracles. What a blessing it is to be born at a time when this is happening and is now being brought to our attention so openly and clearly. How long the faithful waited for this to come about, and now the advent for Christ is over—He is here *among us*; He is here *in us*.

He says we share in the Christ Self. Jesus was a man who realized fully the Christ because He ended the separation between Himself, God, and all his brothers. He united with His brothers and sisters (all of us) and with God as well. He transcended the self of the personality we all make up (the ego) and resurrected into the Self God created (the Christ).

> *Christ is the link that keeps you one with God, (He says) and guarantees that separation is no more than an illusion of despair, for hope forever will abide in Him.*

> *Your mind is part of His, and His of yours. He is the part in which God's answer lies; where all decisions are already made and dreams are over.*

> *He remains untouched by anything the body's eyes perceive. For through Him His Father placed the means for your salvation, yet does He remain the Self, Who, like his Father, knows no sin.*

> *(ACIM; Workbook; "What is the Christ?" Preamble to lessons 271-280)*

Sondra Writes: For me, as perhaps for many of you, Jesus was my childhood teacher. There is no doubt that He gave me my entire spiritual foundation through Christianity. I was raised Lutheran. I was baptized, went to Sunday school, Bible school, Confirmation school, and even to a Lutheran college the first year.

However, I became very confused when my father died when I was 17. They said, "The Lord took him away." I could not resolve this. Were they saying God killed my father? This was intolerable to me. So, I rejected the church because of this and suppressed my love for Jesus. I was wounded. Later I even married an atheist because I was so upset. I tried to go back to church, and I would just cry. It was not until A Course in Miracles came that I got clear how death works, and I forgave the church and opened up to Jesus again.

My mother could not at all understand why I needed a guru like Babaji if I had Jesus. I tried to explain to her that there is no separation between them. They are both in the Holy Spirit's Mind—the Mind of God. Once in India I asked Babaji telepathically this: "What are we going to do about my mother?" That night he gave me a dream.

In the dream, I was looking for a new place to live. I found one I liked very much, but the owner told me it came complete with a roommate and that I had to take it that way or not at all. "Who is that?" I asked. He said: "You will see after you decide."

So that meant I could not find out until after I said, "Yes." This was taking a big chance; but I liked this house very much, so I took it. The next day in the dream I moved in, very curious to see who my roommate would be. I went to the other bedroom next to mine to see who it would be. There He was! It was Jesus Himself appearing to me full on—glowing, alive in all his radiance. I awoke in bliss. Later I said to my mom, "Don't worry Mom. Jesus appeared to me in India." She had no more questions.

THE DIVINE MOTHER

We mentioned Amma as the female guru we follow. She is a manifestation of the Divine Mother's love in our time. Some feel She is the incarnation of the Divine Mother Herself. Anyone who has met Her and received one of Her hugs will attest to a supernatural energy field around Her. This energy of Divine Power is palpable. One can feel it pulsing in them when close to Her. One is transformed by Her hug. It is like She does not even see your ego, but the Holy Self you are. Our last meeting with Amma was here in Washington when She came in 2019, before the pandemic. We stayed in Her energy field for three days in the Marriot Hotel in Arlington where She gave Her darshan and hugs.

We agree that she certainly is one of the most powerful spiritual masters ever to walk the planet. She is right up there with Jesus and Babaji. Although she was a child prodigy, she had a difficult childhood. But she was walking and speaking at six months and singing to Lord Krishna right away.

Her presence is always a potent blessing force, opening us up and infusing our spiritual energy centers. She is a living fountain of grace, and we feel fortunate for our good fortune of having been able to be near her divinity in human form. Go on her website Amma.org and see when her schedule will take her near you next. We do not know when she will resume darshans and now, because of the pandemic, it is forbidden to be in crowds.

Many do consider her to be like a female Christ who always helps release everyone from old wounds and karmic bonds and awaken us to Divine Spirit. Why miss the chance while she is still here? People have seen her levitate and bi-locate. She is like a female form of Babaji also. A few years ago, we went to see her in San Ramone, California. One friend who went with us to see her, leaned over and whispered to us: "This is the highest thing on the whole planet—it is the Source." It was Markus's and his first time with Amma. So, you see, God Herself is appearing in our midst.

Here are some of Her observations:

The moment of revelation that has occurred to many great souls can happen to you as well. Everybody is being prepared to reach this final state of dropping all worldly attachments, all ego. It must happen because that is the final stage of evolution. You cannot avoid it—the final destiny for all souls is the dropping away of every obstruction to peace and contentment. When that moment comes, the ego is dropped, and you won't struggle anymore. You will just bow down and surrender.

Each one of you has the beauty and power of a saint of sage. Each one of you is an infinite source of power. Yet when you see a saint or sage, you recoil. Saying, "No this is for those special people. I can't do it. I have my own tiny little world to bother about and that is enough for me. Divinity is none of my business."—This kind of attitude will never help you to come out of the small, hard shell of your little ego—That is why the Vedanta tells us to contemplate the Vedic dictum: "I am Brahman (Absolute Reality). I am God. I am the Universe. I am absolute power, the totality of consciousness, which makes everything beautiful and full of light and life.

When somebody insults you, he is insulting you from his past, and when you react, you, too are reacting from the past. Both of you have been victims of insults and have made others your victims in your previous lifetimes as well as this lifetime. When others insult you or get angry at you, try to keep your mouth shut, imaging you are in Amma's presence. Try to feel respect for the other person, because in truth, he is doing something good for you. He is teaching you to be silent, to be patient—Feel   deep concern and compassion for him—Try to see that your accuser is suffering from his past wounds. You do not want to hurt a wounded and suffering person. That is cruelty. Be kind and compassionate.

You can raise a hundred objections to the theory of karma—Still the law of karma is operating in your life. You are in its grip.

Children, our actions will return to each one of us, whether one is a believer or non-believer. Karma is like a boomerang. Newborn babies are sometimes physically deformed or mentally retarded. Are such events accidental? No! Each thing that happens in life has a cause. Sometimes the cause is visible; and at other times it is not. Sometimes the cause is to be found in the immediate past— but in some cases it stems from the remote past. Nothing is accidental. Nature is not accidental. Creation is not an accident. Our past is not just the past of this lifetime. The past is also all the previous lifetimes through which we have travelled in different names and forms. We must be alert and careful about what we do today because we do not know what effect it will produce tomorrow.

Your negative feelings will invoke the negative feelings of others. They too will suffer, thereby adding to the storehouse of their karma. Thus, through your anger or selfishness, you have lengthened the chain of someone else's karma also. You are responsible since it happens due to your anger and greed. This is the kind of destruction you do.

Contentment ensues from ego-lessness. And ego-lessness comes from devotion, love, and utter surrender to the Supreme Lord. An ordinary devotee wants to keep his ego, whereas a true devotee wants to die to his ego so that he can live in consciousness of pure innocent love. Dying to the ego makes you immortal. Death of the ego leads you to deathlessness. When the ego dies, you live eternally in bliss. (From Various Books I have by AMMA)

We also relate to the Mother Goddess behind all things. She is the feminine aspect of God and has many forms. She is the Life Force—the original spark of creation. She is the source of all knowledge, the release from delusion, beyond everything. In India they say that there is nothing higher than worship of the Divine Mother. The great Saint Sri Aurobindo said, "Surrender to the Mother is the final stage of perfection for a soul."

Babaji also surrendered to the Divine Mother. When He took samadhi (conscious departure), the last thing He said was, "I am leaving everything in the hands of the Divine Mother." Then He started sending us to Amma. He wanted us to emphasize the Divine Mother energy in our work, to balance out the patriarchy. So that is why we started adding Divine Mother prayers toward the end of every Liberation Breathing/ Breathwork session, plus a mantra to the Divine Mother.

She will bring us to the nurturing, tender aspects of ourselves, which are so needed to solve the problems in the world today. The Divine Mother will give us the solutions both to our personal problems and to our planetary problems. We need to let Her teach us how. We want to avert more catastrophes in our bodies, our relationships, our societies, our countries, and our natural environment. How do we deal with the shadows in ourselves? Logic cannot always find the answer, but the feminine side of our selves is more capable of harmonizing the light and the shadow. Extraordinary changes take place when the Goddess is accepted for women and men alike! I know men whose lives were completely changed by surrendering to Amma or the Divine Mother.

The Goddess, or Divine Mother, leads us in the way of natural law, wisdom, and unconditional love; however, we do not pay enough attention to this aspect of God. That may be because of old beliefs that the Goddess is pagan and heathen. That is most unfortunate, because we then overlook Her beneficial, life-enhancing, and regenerative powers and Her offer for renewal. In Liberation Breathing, She offers us renewal! She offers us liberation from sorrow.

Everything we possess is a gift of the Divine Mother. Presently there is a reawakening of the sacred feminine in the hearts and minds of people throughout the world; and that is partly due to the presence of Ammachi on Earth.

Praise to You Great Mother.
Make our lives a miracle.
Show us what to do and how to do it.
Let us be innocent and receptive like a child.

Make our hearts Your temple.
We pray that people will surrender to You
In Liberation Breathing, as You called it.

THE MASTER IS BEAUTIFUL by MARKUS

Markus wrote a book called *The Master is Beautiful* because he wanted
to demonstrate the absolute value of having a spiritual master guiding
you in your life. He writes this:

> *If you were putting together the "guest list" of a high function of*
> *state, and all the dignitaries of the world were attending from*
> *time immemorial—all the statesmen and stateswomen who had*
> *made a humanistic contribution to the betterment of the human*
> *race were being considered— who would you invite to be the*
> *keynote speaker?*

> *By the same token, if you were putting together a "guest list" for*
> *the most auspicious function of wise people ever held in your*
> *entire life, and you could invite any person from history, or from*
> *your current life, to be the keynote speaker, who would you put on*
> *the short list of the most revered? Who would you place at the*
> *wisest table of honor? Who would you consider to be the ones who*
> *had made the biggest impact on the ethical and moral evolution*
> *of the human race? Or even more pointedly, who of these wise*
> *people made the biggest impact on your life; on your evolution as*
> *a human being; on your clarity as a person, helping you navigate*
> *the life that you have been given?*

> *Consider the nine characters in this book my short list. The Master*
> *Is Beautiful came to me as a title in Bali in December of 2016. We*
> *were there with our group of students on the Bali Quest, staying in*
> *our usual and lovely Nefatari Villas, basking in the natural beauty*
> *that is so much a part of the Balinese life. We were going to sacred*
> *sites—to Tirta Empul, to Besakih, to Ganung Kawi, and attending*
> *the illustrious Balinese dance concerts, and participating in holy*
> *fire ceremonies of the most ancient and authentic kind—and the*

subject of this book came to me. It was a pressing moment of insight that could not be denied or ignored. It came to me that we would be absolutely nowhere in the evolution of our human race without the input of spiritual masters. These are beings who have become the focus of our worship and adoration, yet who have lived their actual lives in the flesh. They imparted their wisdom going through the same trials and everyday tribulations that humans go through, in all space and in all time. They came down into flesh, took an incarnation to uplift humanity to a new level of Truth, Simplicity, Love, and Service. They came to unify, not divide; they came to give, and not take. They came to make compassionate peace in the very midst of the cruelty of war. They came to bring something of the heavenly planes to earth. And they did. And in so doing they became whom I consider, and many others also consider, masters. This action of them coming—and the influence they have had upon the human race and me—is beautiful. Hence, the name of this book emerged—The Master Is Beautiful. (Pages xxviii to xxix by Markus Ray)

This is from the preface to *The Master is Beautiful*. (bit.ly/MasterRay) By reading this book, one can get to know intimately some other spiritual masters who are in our life as well: Tara Singh; Dr. Helen Schucman; Mr. J. Krishnamurti; Morrnah Namalaku Simeona; the spiritual founding fathers of America—Emerson, Thoreau, Whitman, and Lincoln; Sri Muniraj. These masters give us their infinite wisdom. They are blessing us in our life. We hope you will get to know them and have their guidance in your life too, as you stroll down the Aisle for Spiritual Masters in *The Supermarket for a Meaningful Life*.

 **#8.**

AN AISLE FOR VISITING SACRED SITES

Some people have the travel bug. There are roadmaps for wanderlust galore in aisle eight. A sacred site is a place where deep worship has taken place for long periods of time and accumulated a vibration of sacredness that one can palpably feel. We take pilgrimages to these kinds of places. People who visit these kinds of places are uplifted. They can never be the same afterwards. Their spiritual expansion can never again be stuffed back down into a lockdown of limitations.

For years we have been going on *quests*. We would gather people together and travel to a sacred site—stay a week or two. While there we would do breathwork every day. Combining the power of the site along with the inner power of breathwork transformation would make for a great experience of ascension. We call these sacred journeys simply Quests. Ten days of this kind of sacred immersion could seem like ten years. People would go back home expanded, rebooted, and rewired. This is the purpose of any pilgrimage to any holy place—to receive the blessings of the place, and/or from the people who made it sacred originally.

INDIA QUEST

I went to India for the first time in 1977. Leonard Orr and a number of us went there because we were "called." We did not fully know who was calling us, but we had a suspicion we were looking for Babaji, the "Yogi Christ of India" mentioned in Chapter 33 & 34 of *The Autobiography of a Yogi* by Yogananda. It turned out that was truly who was calling us. But it took a little effort to find Him. There were over ten of us in the group with Leonard, and we all agreed to go our separate ways to discover the source of this calling. Then we would meet back in New Delhi in two weeks and compare our notes. This we did. We all had met some powerful spiritual masters. My partner at the time and I went to check out Rajneesh/Osho in Puna. After a while at his ashram, it was clear that was not for me. (Imagine me, who is so into fashion, wearing orange for the rest of my life!) Leonard had met a guru in New Delhi named Abu who was very powerful. But something told us he was not the one either.

One lady in our group had not returned. Missing in action. And one does not find a missing person in India. Too many people and no system to investigate and search out someone lost. So, we had to return to the USA empty handed, without one member in our group.

About six months later, this lady walked into the office of Theta House in San Francisco where we had our rebirthing center, and said, "I found the real Babaji!" I was stunned. I said something kinda stupid like, "How tall is he?" To which she replied, "Which day?" Meaning He changes size depending on His daily purpose. "He is walking around in the foothills of the Himalayan Mountains." And she knew the basic area. So, we all saved up and bought tickets to go back to India as soon as we could.

When we arrived in New Delhi, we met the Guru Abu. He wanted me to stay and be his disciple. I could not decide. Leonard said, "Get your head together and meet me in three days. I am going north to find Babaji." He had given me the name of a town, Haldwani, and a man, Muniraj, who I was to find in that town who would get me the rest of the way. After a couple days of soul searching, I heard the "Aarti" playing in the air. This was a long chant to Babaji. So, I took that as a sign to leave New Delhi and find my true teacher, my sadguru—Babaji.

After an all-day bus ride to Haldwani, full of Indians, farm animals, tires, and what not, I got to Haldwani and started asking people where I could find Muniraj. I thought Haldwani would be a small village. But it was a huge bustling town. "Do you know Muniraj?" I would ask to dozens of people. "No," they would answer. This went on for four hours. When I had almost given up, someone said, "Oh, I think he has a different name here. His name is Trilok Singh, and he owns a feed store down this alleyway."

I thought, "What is a saint doing owning a feed store?" I had a lot of faith back then, so I went down the alley, found the feed store, and knocked on the door. I did not know what to expect after a grueling day of travel and hours of searching. The door opened, and a man in a white silk robe answered, as if illuminated from within. This was Sri Muniraj. the most peaceful being on the planet I had ever met. There was only before this moment and after this moment in my life. I was meeting with Babaji's main disciple. That in itself was what they call a "darshan" in India. I was transformed in his holy energy.

He asked me a few questions. I told him I was searching for Babaji. He told me exactly where to find the river trail nearby that led up to the Haidakhan ashram where Babaji was staying. And then he said a holy blessing of the most powerful kind in my life, "You may go."

I took my backpack and things and hiked up that trail, crossing the river here and there, sometimes with water up to my chest. I wore my passport in a plastic bag around my neck. Finally, I arrived in Haidakhan at the foot of the 108 steps up to the ashram. I ran up the steps with glee, I was so excited to meet my guru. The fact is I ran right past Him. He was wearing a burlap bag with a stalk of straw hanging out of the corner of his mouth, dressed like a farmer. At the top of the steps someone said, "You are supposed to pranam (bow) to the guru." I said, "Well, where is he?" They pointed down the steps to the man in the gunny sack. I thought, how could that be my guru, dressed like that?" I went down to meet Him. He said, "Mrs. Sondra." How did He know my name? Well, He obviously did. Later I found out we had been in seven previous lifetimes together.

This was my first meeting with my master. That night I met Him again in the temple. He was wearing my exact fashion fantasy—silk robes, a pink turban, and the full gloriousness of Lord Shiva Himself. I had finally arrived Home, and I have been His disciple ever since. That was nearly 45 years ago.

Every year since then I have had an *India Quest* in which I take others to Haidakhan with me. It is my passion. We go for the Divine Mother Festival, the Navaratri, that is celebrated in the ashram for nine days and nights. We do this in the Spring now. During this great sequester we have not gone for the past two Springs, due to Covid-19 travel restrictions. We hope to go again in the Spring of 2022. Check it out at bit.ly/IQRay.

Why Go to India?

> *India was the motherland of our race, and Sanskrit the mother of Europe's languages: she was the mother of our philosophy; mother, through the Arabs, of much of our mathematics; mother through the Buddha, of the ideals embodied in Christianity; mother, through the village community, of self-government and democracy. Mother India in many ways is the mother of us all.* –
> Will Durant

Please do not overlook the possibility of going to India, at least once in your life. We have to admit we have a biased opinion, being lovers of India and what it can do for you. In our experience, the minute you set foot on her land, something profound begins to change in you—you can never be the same again. The whole country is like an ashram. The people's main concern is, "How can I love God more?" Even though on the surface, it does not LOOK pure, it will purify you in surprising ways. When you see beyond the dirt, you see so much love, humility, devotion to God and glory that you cannot help but to surrender. Usually, the first thing that happens is the Western mind collapses. It is so different that there is nothing to hang on to. This breaking down of your form is just the beginning. If you go to an ashram, your life will really be turned around.

It was in the ashram that we truly learned to love God. Never have we encountered such an intense stripping of the ego. When we saw what the saints were really like, we were forever challenged to even begin matching their devotion. It is something we long for, and we cannot stop thinking about India. You can come with us on the annual India Quest. We make it easy for you to navigate there and have a marvelous, safe experience. Every year in the Spring we take people to the Himalayan foothills where we celebrate Navaratri for nine days. This is like the final touch. You could call it the tower of ecstasy or maybe you could call it a divine circus!

Markus on India

I went with Sondra Ray to India first back in 1987. I was practicing Sikhism back then, wearing a turban, thinking I was something spiritually special. India Quest definitely wiped that arrogance out of me. We went to Babaji's ashrams in northern India and participated in one of the most ancient festivals on earth—the Navaratri, which is nine days and nights dedicated to honoring the Divine Mother.

Back then I did not fully realize the utmost importance of the Divine Mother. In fact, I did not fully realize much of anything, as I thought what I knew was quite enough. I had not yet been introduced to the importance of acknowledging all that I did not know. And when I finally did, India helped me immensely with this realization. It has an ancient history of renunciation and stepping out of the "self we made up," the so-called ego, into the Self God created, who is the Being we truly are. This renunciation had not yet taken place in me, although I thought that it had.

But India does its work on you. After a couple years it called me back. By then I had met my real teacher, Tara Singh. But I went back to India with Sondra Ray in the fall of 1989. I went back for another round. This time I got the benefit of renunciation and surrender to a power greater than myself. I shaved my head. From then on, I was in Babaji's lineage, even though I did not know it at the time. Nor would I, until I reconnected with Sondra Ray in 2007-8.

If you wish to get on the fast track of spiritual ascension, going to India is one good way to do it. Sondra and I would probably say the *fastest* way to do it. Twelve days in Herakhan can plummet you forward 144 years in your evolution on the outside. Babaji said one day in Herakhan is worth 12 years of progress hacking it out on our own. My experience is that is so. One trip there melted me down and prepared me to meet Tara Singh. Two trips there gave me the ears to hear something else—some wisdom not of my own thought. So, you decide. Go for it and save a lifetime of searching.

BALI QUEST

We can tell you about one culture that is clear on who is running things and that is Bali. The Divine Mother Temple rules. It is on a mountain top and the Balinese government has a place overlooking it.

Having traveled around the world several times, we have never found anything as incredible and wonderful as Bali.

About 40 years ago I went to Bali for the first time. Babaji had just told me to create "The God Training," and I did not have any idea what that was. I knew I needed to push the edge of the envelope on this one. Then I told my staff, "I am going into seclusion in Bali to see what this God Training is all about." This was long before Bali was popular as a spiritual destination. Back then only a few of us knew the sacredness of the "Island of the Gods," as it is sometimes called. So, off I went.

I stayed for a couple of nights in the Oberoi Hotel in Seminyak. Then I moved to Poppy's Cottages on Kuta Beach. One early morning I saw a procession of Balinese women, about a hundred of them, wearing beautiful batik dresses, walking in a perfect row with tall baskets filled with fruits and offerings balanced perfectly on their heads, all moving toward the beach. They laid down long batik cloths on the sand and proceeded to place the baskets of fruit on the cloths as offering to the Gods. I asked someone what they were doing. They said, you are lucky to see this procession. They are doing prayers for the families, and they only do this once a year. I was stunned by the beauty of it all, and the sacredness of how the Balinese live their everyday lives. Holy worship is a way of life for them. Holiness is woven into the very fabric of their being.

I thought, "Where have we gone in the Western world, with all of our technology and materialism?" Nothing compares to the sacredness of Bali and their culture of community worship. No wonder Babaji told me to create The God Training. I went back my cottage and channeled The God Training in a couple of hours. Done deal.

I had a few trainings in Bali after that. And then there were quite a few years I did not go. But once I got together with Markus, I returned with him in 2010, and we have been going back every year since then. We go in December and spend the whole month there. The Bali Quest is always December 3-13. We stay in Ubud and do Liberation Breathing every day. We visit the most sacred sites in Bali and immerse ourselves in the Divine Way that is so prevalently felt everywhere on this Island of the gods. You can come with us if you like.

Markus on Bali

When I went to Bali for the first time in 2010, I could hardly believe there was a place where Divine Beauty was so well expressed. We stayed in the Oberoi Hotel in Seminyak, where the art and culture seemed to come together in perfect harmony. One could also tell that the gods were constantly being honored. One evening there was to be a performance of Legong Dancers for the hotel guests at the outdoor amphitheater. It rained, so they moved the performance into the large, covered dining pavilion. We sat in the dining chairs and watched the most incredible dance I had ever seen.

I felt I had been visited by the Divine Mother Herself, in the form of these young dancers, no older than ten or twelve years. They were masters at this age—masters of Divine movement and beauty unsurpassed in the world I had known. I was speechless.

After that performance I began writing odes to the Divine Mother. I kept this up for four years. Eventually these prose poems became a book, *Odes to the Divine Mother*. (bit.ly/OdesRay) This was only my first encounter with Bali. There were to be many more, and each time I got closer and closer to the heart of the Divine Mother.

We started going to the immortal springs of Thirta Empul, and to the Divine Mother's Besakih Temple on Mount Agung. Each year we would take a group and teach Liberation Breathing and Physical Immortality. We met a Balinese couple who were Babaji devotees, and who performed a havan (fire ceremony) for our group. The whole thing fell into place. We would go to Bali every year and stay a month. It was "getting into our blood" like India. And all was going well in our Quest for the Sacred that we yearned to extend to others. The Bali Quest became an annual stop on our world-wide tour schedule. Always in early December.

We found a set of villas just outside of Ubud that are perfect for our Bali Quest. Each individual villa is walled in with private gardens, swimming pool, verandas, etc. And the staff is attentive, treating us like honored guests. It makes us all feel very high to be there. We teach our classes in our large villa, do rebirthing exchanges in the morning and afternoon, take the group on field trips to sacred sites, and shop in Ubud. People find incredible sacred things to bring back home with them. The Bali Quest is heavenly. We could not do a thing to perfect it even more. It is a gift from the Divine Mother Herself.

ICELAND QUEST

Years ago, when I was leaving India, my teacher, Shastriji, handed me a piece of paper with 108 names of the Divine Mother written on it. He was a poet and a scholar. And he told me to begin reciting these 108 names. The first time I did that in front of my altar in a hotel in Stockholm I received the most incredible knowledge of how to do a wet rebirthing training. I jumped in my bathtub to learn the technique She had given me and practiced it. It was hard, but I learned it and had amazing breakthroughs in my own process as a result.

I shared the technique with my friend, Don McFarland, the founder of Body Harmony, and he came flying out of the tub and said, "This is a stroke of genius!" I said, "It's not from me, it's directly from the Divine Mother." The Mother said the technique should only be taught in natural thermal waters, because this is the Divine Mother Herself. People will feel like they are in the womb of the Divine Mother when they are breathing in natural hot springs. He was so impressed he wanted to take a group to Iceland to try it out. We did. It was amazing breathing in the many thermal springs in Iceland. The Iceland Quest was launched.

Many years went by and when Markus came along, we reinstated this Iceland Quest into our schedule. We take people to the Blue Lagoon, one of the best thermal springs in the world. In this lake of liquid love, we breathe with snorkels and learn the Liberation Technique© that the Divine Mother taught me so many years before. We go in July or August when there is hardly any nightfall in Iceland. It stays light about twenty-two hours a day. We hope you will come with us one day.

THE GLASTONBURY QUEST

Markus writes:

Some say that Glastonbury is the heart chakra of the planet. It is not far from Stonehenge, the ancient prehistoric site of encircled stones, and it is in the part of England where phenomenal and mysterious crop circles have occurred over the years. We have done many trainings in Glastonbury, and in the past few years we have taken a group for the Glastonbury Quest—a retreat dedicated to physical immortality.

Legend would have it that King Arthur is buried in the Glastonbury Abbey grounds. Also, it is said that Joseph of Arimathea, the uncle of Jesus, was there for the mining of tin. Even young Jesus is said to have been there with his uncle at one point. There is a man-made hill called the Glastonbury Tor, which goes back before the Christian era. It has very strong Divine Mother energy, as the Mother was much more worshiped in the ancient times. So, the balance of female / male polarities is superbly felt on the top of the Glastonbury Tor. We take our group up there to breathe in the expansiveness of it all.

All of our trainings and Quests have Liberation Breathing at the center. This is our chosen spiritual practice that helps us move into higher frequencies of loving ourselves and letting go of memories from the past that are holding us back. We go to sacred places that further assist us in going higher. Glastonbury is one of these places. One of the most elated feelings we have ever had is on top of the Glastonbury Tor, looking into the infinity of Spirit, into the myths of Avalon that manifested in the lands below.

#9.

AN AISLE FOR SPIRITUAL HEALING

The first thing to know is that all illness is mental illness. ACIM makes this very clear. We make it very clear in Liberation Breathing—all thought produces form, and all diseases in the body or the mind are preceded by negative thoughts. We are not talking about something psychiatric. It means that all conditions in the body start in the mind. Illness is a conflict in the mind taken out on the body.

Spiritual healing begins with this premise. The body is not "sick," but it is the mind that "thinks" disconnected thoughts from its Source of Love that is sick. And this separation projects symptoms onto the body. The body then, is merely a print-out of the mind that created it. When the mind is focused on its Spiritual Source, healing naturally occurs.

Most separation in the mind from Source Energy comes from three main mental demons: guilt, fear, and anger. Unchecked, they eventually result in death. These are unloving thoughts and emotions that will literally kill you. So, spiritual healing's main function is to clear us of guilt, fear, and anger. You would be surprised how much of these demons are in our minds.

Healing entails replacing fear with love. Love is the main component of Spirit that does the healing. All healing involves this fundamental connection with the Source of Love. It comes from our Divine Connection:

> *Perfect love casts out fear.*
> *If fear exists,*
> *Then there is not perfect love.*
> *But,*
> *Only perfect love exists.*
> *If there is fear,*
> *It produces a state that does not exist.*

> *(ACIM; Text; Chapter 1; Section VI; ¶ 5-6)*

Symptoms are there to get your attention. They are saying to you: "Hey, wake up and look at your thoughts!" It seems like when the symptoms arise, we get in touch with our fear. We might be afraid when we get a diagnosis from a doctor. But the fact is we had the fear before the diagnosis, and even before the illness manifested—and the fear contributed to the disease. So, we need to look at this fear. Where did it come from? Are we willing to let it go?

We also have to look at guilt and anger. These two heavy emotions really go together. Guilt, anger, and resentment are all low emotions that keep us from joy. And the attributes of love abide in peace and joy. We have to be willing to give up guilt, fear, and anger. Perfect love can "cast them out," but we have to be willing to admit our mistake in having them in the first place. We have free will, and we can keep them if we want, but Source Energy would never condemn us for these destructive and low vibrational states. Nor would Source condone them either. The Will of Life would want us to see our perfect sinlessness and original innocence. In this awareness there is joy and peace, so there is no cause for anger or fear.

Guilt always demands some form of *punishment*. Sickness is often punishing yourself for some unspoken guilt, rather than having God punish you.

All forms of sickness are physical expressions of the fear of awakening. (Awakening is joining our will with the universal will of our Creator.) When ACIM says, "God's will for me is perfect happiness," Jesus means perfect. That is *constant joy* that does not have an opposite. Sickness is a defense against the truth of this perfect happiness. As long as we are sick, we are vibrating at a frequency lower that God's will for us. The truth is God's will for us is *perfect love*, and this is total joy, and this is total health, and this is immortality.

Sickness is actually idolatry.

We have to stop pretending sickness and pain are accidents. We made them up! Then we pretend that we did not do that. We pretend that illnesses just happen to us. We fall into the erroneous mindset that sickness, like death, are inevitable. But the truth is we make them up.

> *Miracles enable you to heal the sick and raise the dead because you made sickness and death yourself, and can therefore abolish both. You are a miracle, capable of creating in the likeness of your Creator. Everything else is your own nightmare, and does not exist. Only the creations of light are real.*
>
> *(ACIM; Text; Chapter 1; Section I; ¶ 24)*

These lofty statements are from #24 of the 50 Principles of Miracles in Chapter One of the ACIM Text. They say we made up sickness and death ourselves, and therefore we can abolish them as well. But we need the miracle of a shift in our mind that this is possible. Without faith this is not possible. Doubt would sabotage our ability to heal ourselves with our mind. So, we have to take responsibility for all of our thoughts—the entire content of our minds—and cleanse ourselves of all thoughts that hurt us.

HEALING

The physician is the mind of the patient himself. The outcome is what the patient decides.

Anything you have created, you can uncreate. It is actually less work to heal yourself than to make yourself sick. You really have to work hard indulging in negative thoughts to make yourself sick. It takes a lot of work to hang on to negative thoughts.

Health is an area where everyone needs to claim responsibility for themselves. You DO have power over your body. But from infancy you were told you must check your body with someone else, such as a doctor.

When the ego tempts you to sickness, do not ask the Holy Spirit to heal the body, for this would be merely to accept the ego's belief that the body is the proper aim of healing. The mind is what needs healing. Ask that the Holy Spirit teach you the right perception of the body—through the mind.

Wholeness heals because it is of the mind. All healing involves replacing fear with love. Healing that is of the Holy Spirit always works. Unless the healer always heals by Him, the results will vary. Healing affects our joint will. That is the way the separation is overcome. All things are possible by our joint decision.

Here are some statements from A Course in Miracles that stood out to me regarding healing:

> Health is a natural state relinquishing all attempts to use the body lovelessly.

One thing is not harder to heal than another because nothing is too hard for the Holy Spirit. If the Holy Spirit taught one form of sickness is more serious than another, He would be teaching that one error is more real than another.

Jesus says: Do not set limits on what you believe I can do through you, or you will not accept what I can do for you.

"With God, all things are possible." This statement we were taught as kids in Sunday School. It was also the state motto of Ohio, where Markus grew up.

Do you want the problem, or do you want the answer?

As you become more willing to accept the help of God, by asking for it, you will get it. Nothing will be beyond your healing power because nothing will be denied your simple request.

For healing to happen, the cells must receive and retain more light, and be released from past restrictions, limitations, and imperfections.

All healing is essentially the release from fear. Fear is self-controlled. The correction of fear is our responsibility. Ask for help with the conditions that brought about the fear.

Fear of Healing

Fear of healing: Sudden healing could produce depression in people who have chosen sickness as a way of life and a major way of getting attention. The Holy Spirit will never add to your fear. Pray for removal of the fear of healing first.

But we also have to remember, all healing is temporary until you heal death. We could teach you how to heal anything; but if you don't give up your death urge, you will just make up a new way to kill yourself. As long as you think, death is inevitable, you will create some sickness to prove that you are right.

Most people say: "I won't be happy until I am healthy," but you will be healthy only when you are happy. (Unhappiness is due to loss of connection with the Source.)

Maharishi Mahesh Yogi said this: "Bliss is ultimately the most powerful agent of physiology."

There is a healing force within each of us—a kind of "divine physician." You know this because if you cut yourself, it heals itself. This force is an intelligence that drives the immune system. There is also a condition in the mind in which we have totally released the past and have no charge about it. ACIM says this is a state of complete forgiveness. It calls this the Atonement.

The Atonement heals with certainty. Say this: "I am one with God and I allow the Holy Spirit to undo all my wrong thinking."

Infinite Love and Gratitude transform the molecular structure of water—the same water that makes up the cells. This transformation enables the electromagnetic field of the body to flow freely. When it flows freely, the physical body detoxifies and heals on its own. Infinite Love and Gratitude have the potential to affect the highest of frequencies, which means that they have the power to harmonize the body and restore its balance.

Always remember that *truth cannot deal with errors you want to keep*. So, let's say you have a forgiveness problem, and you don't want to get off it. Well, not even Jesus could heal you if you block the healing by keeping your error. You have free will to reject what you need to change.

Steps to Spiritual Healing

1. Find the cause
2. Confession
3. Spiritual purification practices

To find the cause you need to do the Ultimate Truth Process.

Pick a condition right now you want to work on, such as _____.
Do not answer the below questions by saying, "I don't know." Your true being knows. Your subconscious mind has all the answers.

1. The exact negative thought I had that caused this condition was_____.
2. My payoff for keeping this condition is _____. (A payoff is a neurotic benefit you are getting out of it.)
3. My fear of giving up this condition is_____.
4. If this symptom could talk, what it would say is_____.
5. I will let go of this condition when_____. (What has to happen?)
6. The affirmation I need to think to heal this condition is_____.

Now you need to go to a breathworker or a friend and confess this whole thing to them. This is why breathwork is so effective. You have someone you can trust who will not be judging you, who will take all this in, and see you in your higher Self.

Very Special Prayers:

Here are some very special prayers I used when I was overcoming anorexia after my mother's death.

❖ I know You, Holy Spirit, can and will resolve this problem now by offering me a miracle. I allow this. I allow healing to happen.
❖ I give up my addiction to fear, pain, and death.
❖ I no longer deny you your ability to bestow your blessing of healing on to me.
❖ I decree, I declare, I determine, I decide, I command, and I order, in the name of the I AM PRESENCE, to let go of this condition.
❖ I let go of my power trip of not letting anyone heal me so I could be the king!

❖ I give up my competition with God.
❖ I am united with Jesus, Babaji, and the Divine Mother.

After you have found the cause and done the confession to someone you trust, then it is time to start doing spiritual purification to solve the problem. This is not as hard as you may think. Once you have found the causes, and the thoughts that contributed to the condition, you can turn these thoughts around into affirmations—positive thoughts that reverse your negative thinking. These can now be your new focus. You may still hear the negative thoughts and feelings, but you are dissolving their momentum with the new thoughts.

Here are some of the methods of spiritual purification for healing that we use. We could probably write a whole chapter on each one. On Liberation Breathing, we wrote a whole book, *Liberation Breathing: The Divine Mother's Gift!* (bit.ly/LiberationRay)

1. Liberation Breathing
2. Prayer
3. Affirmations
4. Gratitude
5. Chanting and reciting mantras
6. A Course in Miracles and spiritual books
7. Fasting
8. Solitude
9. Indian sweat lodge
10. Fire purification
11. Body work
12. Acupuncture
13. Ashram and mundan (head shave)

#10.

AN AISLE FOR LONGEVITY (AND THE POSSIBILITY OF PHYSICAL IMMORTALITY)

What if you could live as long as you chose while improving your body and remaining ageless? Would you want that? What if you were able to stay happy and productive and you loved serving humanity and your life still had real meaning? What if you remained healthy with no pain in your body at all? Maybe you would want to stick around. What if you knew death was created by thoughts and you changed those thoughts? Let's say you want to go for it. We are talking about going for it in a body that works, in a life that works, in a life that is more and more meaningful.

First of all, you would have to understand how death works in order to overcome it. Then you would have to handle your unconscious death urge. What is that? It is a conglomerate in your subconscious mind that contains the following:

1. The thought, "I am separate from God"
2. The thought, "death is inevitable"
3. Your personal lie (worst thought about yourself)
4. All anti-life thoughts
5. Your past life memories of dying

6. Your family traditions on death
7. All your guilt, fear, and anger
8. The belief in sin (which is a request for death)
9. Your secret wish to die if you hate your life
10. The belief that things are better on the *other-side*
11. The belief that sickness and death are just a part of life and you cannot do anything about them.

What if you gave up the above thoughts? ACIM says that "Death is a result of a thought called the ego." This is Jesus talking to you. The ego is made up of all your negative thoughts that keep you from remembering you are one with God. We shared this chart before, but here it is again; it is so important. It shows you the difference between the two different thought systems: on the left is the ego's *mortal* thought system; on the right is the Holy Spirit's *immortal* thought system:

MIND MAP

MORTAL MIND— EGO'S Thought System	IMMORTAL MIND— HOLY SPIRIT'S Thought System
Separation	Oneness
Guilt	Innocence
Fear	Love
Pain	Well-Being
Anger	Harmony
Conflict	Peace
Worry	Certainty
Misery	Gratitude
Depression	Happiness
Sickness	Health
Scarcity	Abundance
DEATH	MORE LIFE
I AM NOT!	I AM THAT I AM!

The ego starts with the thought of separation which leads to guilt, which leads to fear, which leads to pain, which leads to suffering, which leads to anger, which leads to more conflict, which leads to sickness, which leads to aging, which leads to death! Some spiritual masters call this the "decent into hell!"

In other words, we kill ourselves with our own thoughts. Therefore, all death is suicide. God does not kill people. God is Life itself. The body dies when the mind can no longer clear itself, and the body has taken on all kinds of degenerations due to mis-thought. People kill themselves by squeezing out the life force by suppressing negative thoughts.

The problem is that we are hypnotized by the thought that *death is inevitable.* Death is also family tradition. You tend to copy your ancestors. But your ancestors did not get enlightened. What if you did?

Let's look at the causes of aging and death again:

1. INVALIDATION OF YOUR PERSONAL DIVINITY: You do that by having negative thoughts about yourself—such as, "I am not good enough," "I am bad," "I am weak," "I can't make it," or whatever is your actual personal lie. You are then saying, "I am not one with God, I am (whatever negative thought about yourself you put there)." That invalidates your Divinity.

2. FALSE RELIGIOUS THEOLOGY: The belief that you are a sinner might be something you heard a lot in church and in past lives. ACIM says that is never true. If you believe in sin, you are requesting death as a punishment. Many believe that somewhere else is better. But when you die you do not automatically go to a higher place. Consciousness seeks its own level. You could be in Heaven here if you are enlightened.

3. LACK OF IMMORTALIST PHILOSPHY: Nobody told you that you had a choice to do something else besides die. And yet immortals are in the Bible. Some lived for 900 years. Some ascended. How did they do that? If one can do it, others can do it.

4. BELIEF SYSTEMS: You have been programmed by medicine that at a certain age, your body will fall apart. And you have believed that you are going to run out of energy at some point. And you have believed that you will eventually get some disease that you cannot conquer. You have believed that you cannot control what happens to your body. You have believed that you will eventually go down-hill.

5. FAMILY TRADITIONS: You have been programmed to think that you will die like your ancestors did. You might have programmed yourself to die, for example, at the same age as your grandparents. You may copy your own parents' deaths.

6. OVEREATING AND ADDICTIONS: It is a well-known fact that if you eat less, you live longer. But we have been programmed to believe we *must* eat three meals a day. You may be very careless about how you eat. We all know that addictions could kill us. This goes without saying. Food can be a self-destructive addiction.

7. ANGER AND NON-FORGIVENESS: Anger is very dangerous for your body and causes all kinds of disease. Most people also go to the grave with accumulations of non-forgiveness. When you don't forgive, you remain angry, and anger can kill you.

8. UNRESOLVED TENSION AND UNRESOLVED BIRTH TRAUMA: If you have a lot of tension in your body, you obviously would not want to stick around. One of the big causes of tension is suppressed birth trauma. Most people never work out their birth trauma. That, however, was one of the reasons we created rebirthing. You can breathe it out. You feel totally different when you do that.

9. UNCONSCIOUS DEATH URGE: That is your wish to die if you hate your life, and all your programming on death which we mentioned above.

Clearing these causes of aging and death would obviously produce a new result in your body. It is not hard. It is harder to keep all these things going. Releasing them is fun and it is part of your spiritual path to enlightenment.

WHAT ARE THE RESULTS OF THE DEATH URGE?

We list them here:

1. Fear and anxiety
2. Inhibited creativity
3. Illness
4. Aging
5. Blocked wisdom
6. Anger
7. Fatigue
8. Depression
9. Helplessness
10. Failure
11. Anything out there not thriving in your space
12. War (group death urge)

Some people will say to us, "I don't have a death urge. I want to live." However, unless your parents were both immortal yogis, you have been programmed to die. Find out what is your programming. When did you *think* you were going to die and of what condition?

In case you think this discussion is incredulous, listen to what Jesus says in ACIM:

> No one can die unless he chooses death. What seems to be fear of
> death is really its attraction.
> (ACIM; Text; Chapter 19; Section IV; C ¶1)

There you have it.

Some people tell us that they would not even want to live a long time because it is too painful. However, the reason they are in pain is because they did not clear the wish to die. That is what causes the pain. One publisher told us they did not think it was a good idea for mankind to try to overcome death. I suppose they would have nothing to say to some Sequoia trees that are three-thousand years old!

So, let's say you decided you want to experience longevity and you want to be free of pain, sickness, and aging. You then need to imagine that you can live as long as you choose. That is the first step. Physical immortality is the ability to live as long as you choose while improving your body.

It is the merging of body, mind, and spirit. A yogi in India gave us a quick version of it. He said the following:

- ❖ *SPIRIT is that which cannot be destroyed.*
- ❖ *MIND is condensed spirit.*
- ❖ *BODY is condensed mind.*
- ❖ *Therefore, BODY IS UTMOST SPIRIT.*

ACIM would agree with this. It says you are not a body. There is a lesson which states, "I AM SPIRIT." (ACIM; Lesson #97)

Jesus was already teaching this in the Bible. Look at John 8:51:

> *I tell this truth: Whoever holds fast to my teachings never enters the grave.*

Could any talk be plainer?

Critics might say: "Isn't this all just an ego trip?" The answer to that question is this: NO. The purpose of it would be a selfless dedication to a mission of divine service. You are not doing it so you can brag that you are 150 or 200 years old. You are sticking around to serve and you want to stay healthy to do that.

The way to stay healthy is to understand this philosophy.

WHAT ARE THE ADVANTAGES OF THIS PHILOSPHY?

❖ *Increased health*
❖ *Increased energy*
❖ *Increased creativity*
❖ *Increased quality of life*
❖ *Increased potential for regeneration*
❖ *Increased fun*
❖ *Increased joy*

Imagine feeling better than you have ever felt. In order to do so, you have to master the philosophy, the psychology, and the physiology of it.

1. *Philosophy: You study the books available. The main point of the philosophy is this: You already are pure Spirit.*

2. *Psychology: You have to unravel your own personal death urge. You do this through a technique like Liberation Breathing.*

3. *Physiology: You have to be aware that your body is an energy system. You start to notice what foods increase your energy and which decrease your energy. You start to notice which people increase your energy and decrease your energy. You start to notice which places increase your energy and which decrease your energy. You obviously avoid that which decreases your energy.*

STEPS TO PHYSICAL IMMORTALITY

1. *Immerse yourself in the philosophy. Suggestion: Read books on this subject for one whole year.*
2. *Unravel your personal death urge. Commit to Liberation Breathing as a life-long spiritual path.*
3. *Body mastery: Learn to heal any disease, and better yet, stay in a state where you never get sick, which IS possible if you have the right thoughts.*
4. *Stay in a state of Love, Praise and Gratitude.*

5. *Stay in a state of Knowing; having certainty.*
6. *Death of the ego. Become enlightened.*

In case you still think this subject is crazy or impossible, let us share with you what the masters say: In the teacher's manual of ACIM there is a section called "What is death?"

Death is the central dream from which all illusions stem. Is it not madness to think of life being born, aging, losing vitality, and dying in the end? We have asked this question before, but now we need to consider it more carefully. It is the one fixed, unchangeable belief (and a belief is just thoughts you keep on thinking) of the world that all things in it are born only to die. This is regarded as the "way of nature" not to be raised to question, but to be accepted as the "natural" law of life. The cyclical, the changing, the unsure, the undependable and the unsteady, waxing and waning in a certain way on a certain path—all this is taken as the will of God. And no one asks if a benign Creator could will this.

In this perception of the universe as God created it, it would be impossible to think of Him as loving. For who has decreed that all things pass away, ending in dust and disappointment and despair, can but be feared. He holds your little life in his hand, but by a thread, ready to break it off without regret or care, perhaps today. Or, if he waits, yet is the ending certain. Who loves such a god knows not of love, because he has denied that life is real. Death has become life's symbol. His world is now a battleground, where contradiction reigns and opposites make endless war. Where there is death, is peace impossible?

Death is a symbol of the fear of God. If death is real for anything, there is no life. Death denies life. But if there is realty in life, death is denied. No compromise in this is possible. There is either a god of fear of One of love. God did not make death because He did not make fear. And the last to be overcome will be death. (ACIM; MT; 27.)

Hindu Scholar, Haridas Chaudhuri, in his book *Being, Evolution and Immortality* explains that immortality transcends the view of the body as a burden:

> *The concept of immortality implies a harmonization of the entire personality and a transformation of the physical organism as an effective channel of expression of higher values. This may be called material immortality.*
>
> *There are some mystics and spiritual seekers who strengthen and purify their bodies just enough to be able to experience the thrilling touch of the Divine. They use the body as a ladder, by which the pure spiritual level—the domain of immortality—is to be reached. On attaining that level, the body is felt as a burden, as a prison house, as a string of chains that holds one in bondage. Dissociation from this last burden of the body is considered a sine qua non for total liberation. Continued association with the body is believed to be the result of the residual trace of ignorance. When the residual trace of ignorance is gone, the spirit is set free from the shackles of the body.*
>
> *The above view is based upon a subtle misconception about the purpose of life and the significance of the body. The body is not only a ladder that leads to the realm of immortality, but also an excellent instrument for expressing the glory of immortality in life and society. It is capable of being thoroughly penetrated by the light of the Spirit. It is capable of being transformed into what has been called the "Diamond Body." As a result of such transformation, the body does not appear any more to be a burden on the liberated self. It shines as the Spirit made flesh. It functions as a very effective instrument for creative action and realization of higher values in the world. It is purged of all inner tension and conflict. It is liberated from anxiety of repressed wishes. It is also liberated from the dangerous grip of the death impulse born of self-repression. Mystics who look upon the body as a burden suffer from anxiety of self-repression and the allurement of the death wish.*

Material immortality means decisive victory over both of these demons. It conquers the latent death instinct in man and fortifies the will to live as long as is necessary as a channel of expression of the Divine. It is increasingly channeled into ways of meaningful self-expression. Under the guidance of the indwelling light of the Eternal, it produces increasing manifestation of the Spirit in Matter.

From Satprem's **The Mind of the Cells:**

Our question is really that of death. As long as the physical reality of the coffin or the funeral pyre is not changed, nothing will be changed. (p. 63)

Death is not inevitable. It is an accident which has always happened until now. We have gotten into our heads to overcome this accident. Absolute fearlessness is required because at every step at every second, you must wage a war against everything that is established. (p. 69)

Death comes from distortion of Consciousness, nothing more. (p. 108)

Of course, the immortality of this old body is not the goal. That would not be worth the trouble. The new consciousness must gradually change the modalities of its body, change this corporeal rigidity into a new flexibility. (p. 112)

I have the feeling that death is only an old habit now, it is no longer a necessity. It is only because the body is still unconscious—this tremendous collective "suggestion" weighs on you. (p. 190)

Couldn't it be that one day suddenly the vibration of truth might come through the mesh of our web and cancel out, make unreal throughout the world, the horror, the pain, the death, and that we might awaken in a new world—in which the old laws of death will not make any sense, and will vanish like a futile dream? A sudden change that would catch us so unprepared that we would drop our entire arsenal and find ourselves bursting with immense laughter? (p. 119)

The Immortality of Man from Baird Spaulding's *Life and Teachings of the Masters of Far East; Vol 1*

Through the power of process of thought we can transmute and evolve our bodies, or our outer conditions and surroundings through recognition of Christ Consciousness within ourselves, so that we will never experience death nor any change called death. This is done wholly through man's power to visualize, idealize, conceive and bring forth that which he gazes upon. This is done by first knowing or perceiving or having faith that the Christ is within ourselves; seeing the true meaning of Jesus' teachings; holding our body one with God, made in the image and likeness of God and merging that body into the perfect God body just as God sees us. We are born again truly of and in the Spirit kingdom of God. (p. 60)

There is a striking resemblance between the life and teachings of Jesus and those of these Masters. They have so overcome death that many of them now living are over 500 years of age, as was conclusively proved by their records. (p. 3)

The Door of Everything by Ruby Nelson

The last and greatest evil to be removed from my precious planet earth is Satan's evil, death. Death never has been and never will be the way I call my children home. (p. 166)

Death comes into existence along with all the unhappy experiences as a result of mis-thinking. (p. 169)

Your soul yearns to be exalted by the vibration of the Ascension Attitudes so it can travel the way of Saints. In order to travel this highway, it needs a body which overcomes destructive earth vibrations and is transmuted into light. (p. 167)

It is true that life is everlasting regardless of how many times the body dies. It is true that the soul lives on and creates a new body for itself. But it is also true that the soul is endowed with wisdom, and it knows that death of the body is out of harmony with my universal law of life. (p. 167)

FROM THE BIBLE

There shall not be any more death. (Revelation 2:4)

The law of the wise is a foundation of life to depart from the snares of death. (Proverbs 13:14) (Note: the snares are all negative thoughts that bring on old age, ugliness, sickness and finally death.)

If a man keeps (lives) *my sayings: He shall never see death. (John 8:51)*

The last enemy that shall be destroyed (in a man's life) *is death. (I Corinthians 15:26)*

For the carnally minded is death: but to be spiritually minded is life and peace. (Romans 8:6)

Follow me and let the dead bury the dead. (Matthew 8:22)

With God all things are possible. (Matthew 19:26)

But I tell you this truth, there be some standing here, which shall not taste of death. (Luke 9:27)

So then, are YOU determined to hold onto old beliefs about the inevitability of death and the aging process or will you join the biologists, biochemists, gerontologists, geneticists, and other scientists who, whatever their divergent views and fields of research, offer one basic and common prediction: You will have the opportunity to live longer than you have ever supposed.

We are not talking about more years spent in old age or being senile longer. What we are talking about is the idea of *youthing*. Longevity without success, health, and bliss is not desirable. Just to reiterate: your death urge is the cause of your misery.

From *Snoopy* by Charles Schultz:

The secret of staying your age is to find an age you like and stick with it.

THE ANTI DEATH MANTRA

Om Tryambakam Yajaa Mahe
Sugandhim Pushtim Vardhanam
Urvaar Rukamiva Bandhanaan
Mrityor Mukshiya Mamritaat

Affirmations:

- ❖ I am alive now, therefore my life urges are stronger than my death urges. As long as I continue strengthening my life urges, I will go on living in health and youthfulness.
- ❖ Life is eternal. I am life. My mind is the thinking quality of life itself and is eternal. My physical body is also eternal; therefore, my living flesh has a natural tendency to live forever in perfect health and youthfulness.
- ❖ My body totally renews itself as long as I like.

ASCENSION

Ascension is rising to a higher and higher level of frequency where your biology actually ascends.

The 3rd dimension ends in death. (What you see on TV)
The 4th dimension is the New Age. (Thought produces effects)
The 5th dimension is Christ Consciousness (Grace liberates us)

So, ascension is an increased frequency of vibrations and Liberation Breathing and other spiritual practices help you to ascend. But you cannot ascend with the density of fear, guilt, or anger.

This whole process we are going through with the pandemic is an opportunity to ascend.

 # #11.

AN AISLE FOR RELATIONSHIPS

I once read a study by the Hazelton Clinic. They were talking about the stages of a relationship. This was research on average Americans.

Stage 1: Dream stage (lasts 6 weeks to 6 months)
Stage 2: Disillusionment stage (lasts up to 2 years)
Stage 3: Misery stage (lasts up to 30 years!)
Stage 4: Enlightenment stage
Stage 5: Mutual respect

My problem with this study is this: By the time you get to that enlightenment stage and mutual respect, you are too old to enjoy it. Therefore, how do we jump from the dream stage to the enlightenment stage and skip 30 years of misery? That is why we are doing this work— to get that answer. The problems in most relationships are psychological, but the solutions are mostly spiritual.

Step One: Clear up your relationship with God and the Divine in your life.
Step Two: Watch all your other relationships clear up too.

If you want your personal relationships to work, you must get clear on your relationship with God. When you are clear about who or what God is to you, then you will have all the help you need for your relationships. If you are not clear about God, you might tend to blame God for your troubles; you may even think God is out to punish you. Or worse, you may think God does not exist, and that you just made yourself up.

God is the Source from which everything and everyone arises. You could call that the Source of Life. If you don't have a good relationship with the Source, how can you have a good relationship with people? How can you love someone when you don't love the Source? Maybe you tried to run away from God like I did once. I, Sondra, was mad at God about my father's death so I ended up marrying an atheist. Of course, that did not work.

God is the great affirmative that always says *Yes* to your thoughts. God is like energy added unto your thoughts. So, you have to have good thoughts, or you will get more of your negativity. All your relationships are determined by you; you can have them however you want them, because God gave you free will.

From the very beginning, your relationship will work the best while centered in the Divine. Only a relationship that is centered, and has God as the primary factor, will be able to deal with all the life challenges. Both beings must be plunged individually into a deep and passionate devotion of the Beloved, by whatever name they know the Beloved. In other words, from the very beginning it must be centered in the Divine.

Your relationship should be like a prayer you offer to the world. It should be a relationship that is undertaken in the conscious presence of the Divine for the Divine's great work in the universe. Only a relationship centered in God will be able to rise above the problems of life. This holy purpose is what will give it meaning.

The next step is to see the relationship as a contribution to the transformation of the world. This relationship should be based on a united vision of loving and Divine Service to the world. This is called an evolutionary relationship by Andrew Harvey. He says that service helps us find the ability to stay passionately in love with our partner. Service nurtures others to bring even greater love back to the relationship.

Harvey states this: "If we continue to have a vision of relationships as purely personal, purely private, and something that we cultivate only for our own pleasure, we will keep feeding the tragic narcissism that is ravaging the planet on every level." (p. 9 of *Evolutionary Love Relationships* by Andrew Harvey) I can honestly say this is the very best advice. That is what we ourselves have now and it works perfectly.

We learn generosity of gifting by serving and then we can practice more and more gifting in our relationship. You can be excited, thrilled, and enriched by something you are doing together in the world.

Our Master Babaji says the same: Truth, Simplicity, Love and Service to humanity are the four pillars to happiness. We have to discover something in ourselves we have to give. When we give out of the joy of service, our lives are enriched in human terms. Our love is increased.

Ralph Waldo Emerson said, "Problems cannot be resolved by personal solutions." When we step out of the personal for greater action of the impersonal, we invoke Infinite Intelligence to help us.

The next step as we said above is to be enlightened. Once both parties in a relationship are enlightened, anything can be solved. Until then, it is often difficult, because of negative thinking. Your thoughts produce your results even though you are no longer consciously aware of them. Yes, you might know it is important to think positively all the time—but how about your unconscious negative thoughts?

Both of you need a way to clear those. That is why we love Liberation Breathing as it brings the unconscious to the conscious. In other words, if something terrible happens to you or your mate, you might have trouble taking responsibility for creating that situation if you are unaware of the negative thoughts in the subconscious mind that attracted that. Enlightened couples know how to process their results and keep from creating negative results again and again.

An example of what I mean is this: A thought from birth that can destroy relationships for a woman might be, "Men hurt me." That could be a preverbal thought a baby girl formed when the doctor slapped her to breathe. This thought could begin to produce results early on. Maybe in kindergarten boys act out this belief by knocking her down or even hitting her. She is teased by boys in grade school, and it hurts her. Then in high school she starts dating boys and finds herself jilted. This certainly hurts. She enters adulthood certain that men will hurt her. Maybe she will even create an abusive husband. Or maybe she will create her husband running off with her best friend. All this because she did not even realize she had the subconscious thought, "Men hurt me." Enlightened couples know how to locate negative thoughts in their subconscious and process them out.

Obviously, women act out men's thoughts in just the same way. A thought originating at birth for many men is, "Women want to suffocate (kill) me." A woman may act that out by being too maternal and overprotective. Men may feel trapped because of that thought. The way to rid ourselves of these destructive subconscious thoughts is to identify them by careful examination, and use breathing techniques and affirmations to uproot and heal the negative thoughts.

A Course in Miracles defines enlightenment as choosing the Holy Spirit's thought system over the ego's thought system. An enlightened couple knows the difference and is vigilant against the ego. Again, the ego is based on separation, the result is guilt, fear, pain, struggle, misery, suffering, anger, depression, sickness, and death. The Holy Spirit's thought system is unity, oneness, innocence, love, joy, peace, harmony, health, and more life.

If you are operating in an enlightened paradigm, you will understand and honor the following statements and how each applies to your relationship:

> ❖ *You will attack what does not satisfy, and thus you will not see you made it up. (ACIM; Text; Chapter 30; Sec IV; ¶1)*

❖ *Beware of the temptation to perceive yourself unfairly treated. (ACIM; Text; Chapter 26; Sec X; ¶4)*

❖ *Only you can deprive yourself of anything. (ACIM; Text; Chapter 11; Sec IV; ¶4)*

❖ *And everything that seems to happen to me I ask for and receive as I have asked. (ACIM; Text; Chapter 21; Sec II; ¶2)*

In other words, life presents to me what my thoughts are. Being enlightened has to do with taking responsibility for all the results in your life all the time. "Your results are your gurus," we say in the LRT (Loving Relationships Training). ACIM will tell you that all trials are lessons you failed to learn previously. You are always given another chance to *choose once again* and do better.

A Course in Miracles teaches us that we must immediately dedicate our relationships to the Holy Spirit if we want them to work. Otherwise, we will be stuck in our ego and the relationship could be hell.

HOLY VS. UNHOLY RELATIONSHIPS

ACIM talks about "special" relationships. A special relationship (unholy) is based on the assumption that something within us is lacking and therefore we have special needs. To satisfy these needs we come to believe that another individual is capable of giving us that which is missing in ourselves. A conviction of our own littleness lies at the heart of every special relationship. We regard one individual (our mate) as more special than anyone else, more valuable than ourselves, and even more precious than God. We are limiting our love to one small segment of the sonship. And somewhere inside of us we are aware that we have forsaken the totality of the Son-ship and this produces guilt. Guilt demands punishment. So, then we punish ourselves and things get worse. The special relationship is a compelling distraction we use to obscure our attraction to God the Father. We then deny our need for God.

ACIM says the special relationship is the ego's chief weapon to keep us from God.

An unholy relationship feeds on differences, each partner perceives that his mate possesses qualities or abilities he does not have. Each partner enters into such a union with the idea of completing themselves and robbing the other. They each remain in the relationship only until they decide that there is nothing left to steal and then they move on. In an unholy relationship, whatever reminds a person of past grievances attracts them. Partners in this kind of relationship are not there out of a wish to join with their mate in spirit. Such people are not even attempting to join with the body of their mate. Instead, they seek a union with bodies of those who are not there—such as father or mother. (ACIM; Text p. 331)

There is even what the Course calls a "special hate relationship." This relationship is clearly one of anger and attack. In this arrangement one person becomes the focus of our anger, and we hold on to everything they have done. This relationship wreaks vengeance on the past. It holds the past against us. And it involves a great amount of pain, anxiety, despair, guilt, and attack. It uses the partner as a scapegoat.

In a *special love relationship,* your mate becomes your savior. In the *special hate relationship,* they become your enemy.

In sharp contrast to a special (unholy) relationship, a holy relationship rests on solid ground. Each partner has looked within himself and perceives nothing inherently lacking. Accepting his own completion, he finds pleasure in extending it, and so joins with another who is also whole and complete. They come together and share their light with the world. Because they have both evolved to the same degree, no great differences exist between them. This relationship contains and reflects Heaven's holiness. Completion comes from union with God and from the extension of that union with others.

A holy relationship requires that both partners strive together toward a common goal. When two people share the same goal and they search for the love of God, a healing takes place. Giving flows endlessly. A light emanates outward, illuminating to the world. In a holy relationship, seemingly difficult situations are accepted as blessings. Instead of obsessively criticizing one's partner, forever pointing out any imperfections that must be changed, there is a pull toward praise and appreciation. Having created an atmosphere of praise, love, and gratitude, each partner may begin to perceive the Christ in each other.

A SACRED PARTNERSHIP

In a sacred partnership, each partner is equally committed in assisting the other in his or her spiritual growth. Each must understand that the most profound reason they are together is for the evolution of their souls. This creates a whole new vibration between them.

A relationship should be about growth and movement. A relationship is a process; in that process, the couple should celebrate changes in themselves that are stimulated by the other. They should not resent the fact that the relationship is stimulating them to make changes. Each should want the other to become all that he or she can be. In other words, you should not hold yourself back in any way, nor should you allow the other to hold you back. In fact, you should use the support of your mate to help propel you forward, to advance. Each should enjoy empowering the other, but neither should give away their power. Don't sell out. Work it out.

We are talking about making intimacy as a path. Intimacy leads to transformation. The power of intimacy brings up all of one's fear to be processed. There is such a thing we call *spiritual intimacy*. This is the foundation for all intimacy, even sexual. We wrote a whole book on this subject because it is so important: *Spiritual Intimacy: What You Really Want from Your Mate.*

Spiritual intimacy begins with the premise that we are together for Self-awakening. And this self is shared in a communion between us that is sacred. All that we do together has this sacred vibration of pure joy. The vibration of our relationship itself is one of holiness. Our minds are focused together on this inner awakening that puts us in touch with Higher Realities. Not only are we together for the evolution of our souls, but we are together for this final ascension, this awakening.

THE NEW PARADIGM IS A PARADIGM OF JOY AND A HOLY RELATIONSHIP

It begins with total self-esteem. You have to love yourself and be happy with yourself alone first. If you love yourself, you will give others the opportunity to love you; and you will know that you deserve it. Loving from need does not work. Where need ends, true love begins. If you have self-esteem, you will attract someone else with self-esteem; and two people with self-esteem can handle a loving relationship, as love is not a threat to them. Self-esteem is ultimately self-approval.

It is very easy to attract a mate if you think you can. If you understand metaphysics, the days of worrying and hoping are over. There is such a thing as the universal metaphysical law of attraction. It always works if you let it in. Some people walk around saying they can't find the right mate, or many other negative thoughts are going on in their subconscious. If you have asked for a mate and you have not received one, you are then blocked, and it would be helpful to have a private Liberation Breathing session with us or another breathworker to see where you are blocked in your mind.

KEYS TO FINDING A MATE

1st KEY: Not to need one in order to be happy.

2nd KEY: Pray to God and the masters to make it happen. We call this the Cosmic Dating Service. Say to God, "If I am not ready, make me ready."

3rd KEY: Put your entire energy into your spiritual path and service work.

Then, you will attract a mate who can handle a holy relationship.

Three Types of Mating:

In the book *The Esoteric Philosophy of Love and Marriage* by Dion Fortuna, the author states that there are three different ways couples join:

1. Through ordinary attractions of sexual ties
2. By renewing karmic ties
3. According to higher cosmic laws

The Sexual Tie: Unfortunately, many people hurry into permanent mating urged on by physical desire. People often erroneously rationalize their feelings by idealizing the object of their desire. Suddenly one day they realize they have bound themselves for life to a person who is incapable of satisfying any of their other needs. Misery follows. One's judgment can be clouded over easily. Some teachers say you should wait nine months before having sex and use that time to develop the friendship.

The Karmic Tie: Bonds based on karma are less easy to distinguish. Karmic ties are rooted in attractions experienced in past lives. For a full discussion on this phenomenon, we recommend you read *You Were Born Again to Be Together* by Dick Sutphen.

The Cosmic Tie: This is the most profound and potent tie. It is a partnership entered by two individuals for the purpose of performing a special service. The partners in this union do not choose each other. They offer themselves in service to the master on the inner planes. They are mated by the master with attention to their qualities and capacities. The pair opens a channel. Divine forces flow through them with astounding power, magnetizing them and their surroundings. This is what was arranged for us by Babaji when I asked Him to find me my perfect mate that fit the mission. He sent me Markus.

Dion Fortuna advises that before we mate seriously, we should consult a gifted psychic and or astrologer. The other interesting thing in this book was the fact that she stated if you have sex with someone who does not match your plane (such as someone who is on a lower plane) that can bring you way down and destroy all the good you have gathered from years of spiritual practices.

A typical priority list in the old paradigm for attracting mates goes something like this:

1. There must be sexual chemistry
2. We must share similar interests
3. We must share similar religious backgrounds

The spiritual masters recommend the reverse:

1. Soul unity is most important
2. Sharing similar interests
3. Sexual chemistry

THE WILLINGNESS TO CLEAR: SELF-ANALYSIS

Enlightened couples still have problems like everyone else, but the way they handle them is totally different. They apply self-analysis techniques to their relationship. They break old destructive patterns in their relationships and create new, healthy models or paradigms. They know that their relationship is central to their spiritual path, and they are committed to doing whatever it takes to stay on track. They take responsibility for anything that is not pure joy, and they correct it.

We see many couples in which one partner is willing to practice self-analysis and the other is not. This combination rarely works because they end up in totally different frequencies. The partner willing to process usually starts to grow a lot faster than the other, and they end up not sharing similar levels of commitment to the awakening process. If you find yourself in this situation, you need to look at why you created this situation for yourself and if it is right to stay.

The spiritual master, Yoganada, has always said that self-analysis is the key to the mastery of life. He has also stated that without self-analysis, man leads a robot-like life.

People who never analyze themselves are like mechanical products of the factory of their environment. They are preoccupied with breakfast, lunch, and dinner, working, and sleeping and being entertained. They don't know what or why they are seeking, nor why they never realize complete happiness. —*Yogananda*

The Bible says, "Be perfect even as God is perfect." That is an assignment. The only way to have a perfect relationship is if both people are willing to experience their own perfection. To experience your own perfection, you must release the ego's thought system. And in a relationship, you have to both be committed to this. If there is a resistance to self-analysis, find out why. A very simple example of self-analysis is this:

1.   My negative thoughts which created this situation are:
2.   The desired result outcome of this situation is:
3.   The new thoughts or affirmations I need to think about in order to achieve this desired outcome are:

DEFINING A LOVING RELATIONSHIP

The loving part of your relationship is already handled. You are love and your partner is love. You just have to remove the blocks to the awareness of love's presence. But the relating part of your partnership is where the *game* comes in. You invent or try out a game such as, "Let's move in together," or, "Let's live separately and see each other three times a week," or, "Let's just be friends for a few months before having sex," or, "Let's get married."

If you don't like the set up, you can change the game. It is important not to impose the exact form or pacing from a previous relationship onto your new one. Each new person has a history, unique patterns, fears, and desires. One thing to remember is that you are in charge of how you want your relationship to look and function. How you do this has to bring the ultimate joy to both of you.

THE BIG PROBLEMS IN RELATIONSHIPS

MARKUS WRITES ABOUT FEAR

Fear, anger, and guilt are the biggest saboteurs in all relationships. We cannot relax, and therefore we cannot really love in these alternative states of being. Problems cannot be solved in these vibrational fields. In fact, the momentum of a problem is perpetuated using anger, fear, or guilt. We form our battlelines along these emotions.

A Course in Miracles would say there are only two options in our emotional bag to choose from—love or fear. And they are mutually exclusive, so we are in one or the other. We cannot be in both. This is a sobering realization. Then it goes on to say:

> *Fear is not justified in any form.*
> *(ACIM; Lesson #240)*

Why is that? Few of us can say we have never felt fear. Why would that be unjustified. It requires a deep answer we may not be willing to hear. ACIM makes it clear we can identify with only one of two different "selves." There is a self we made up and a Self who God Created. The self we made is based on thinking we are a body, and this body can experience the threats of the world, and we must protect it from danger and demise. This is the world in which we live—one of danger and twists and turns of fate beyond our control—furthermore, there is the "fact" that eventually death will snuff us out for good. In this world, fear seems very justified. But our larger identity is Spirit. This dimension of Being is not subject to the conditions of a physical identification and existence. Spirit is that which cannot be harmed or threatened in any way. It is the realm of absolute Love. We are that. Therefore, we are immortal, deathless, unassailable in any way. In this Self God created there truly is nothing to fear.

It is a matter of training ourselves to identify with the Spirit in our day-to-day existence. It is a matter of attention and focus—to what do we give our attention?

> *Begin these happy exercises with the words the Holy Spirit speaks to you, and let them echo round the world through Him:*
>
> Spirit am I, a holy Son of God, free of all limits, safe and healed and whole, free to forgive, and free to save the world.
>
> *Expressed through you, the Holy Spirit will accept this gift that you received of Him, increase its power and give it back to you. (ACIM; Lesson #97)*

Knowing that we are "free of all limits" would alleviate fear. This would require we have a different way of looking at ourselves and our world. One in which peace is valued above all else. One in which forgiveness rests upon all things. We would also have to handle any anger and guilt.

ANGER

Here is what the gurus say on the subject:

Guru Mai: "It is said that if you are a true ascetic, you are completely devoid of anger. If there is any trace of anger in you, you are called a scoundrel, not an ascetic.
"A great being will go to any extent to remove the fire of anger. The greatness of a saddhu monk is that he can drop something once he knows he has had it."

Dalai Lama: "We lose control of our mind through hatred and anger. If our minds are dominated by anger, we will lose the best part of human intelligence—wisdom. Anger is one of the most serious problems facing the world today."

Amma: "Anger and impatience will always cause problems. Suppose you have a weakness of getting angry easily. Once you become more normal again, go and sit in the family shrine room or in solitude and regret and repent your anger and sincerely pray to your beloved deity or Mother Nature, seeking help to get rid of it. Try to make your own mind aware of the bad outcome of anger. When you are angry at someone you lose all your mental balance. Your discriminative power completely stops functioning. You say whatever comes in your mind and act accordingly.

"You may even utter crude words. By acting and thinking with anger, you lose a lot of good energy. Become aware that these negative feelings will only pave the way for your own destruction."

Jesus of ACIM: "Anger is *never* justified. Attack has *no* foundation. It is here escape from fear begins and will be made complete. Here is the real world given in exchange for dreams of terror. For it is on this forgiveness rests, and is but natural...

"Pardon is *always* justified. It has a sure foundation. You do not forgive the unforgivable, nor overlook a real attack that calls for punishment. Salvation does not lie in being asked to make unnatural responses which are inappropriate to what is real. Instead, it merely asks that you respond appropriately to what is not real by not perceiving what has not occurred."
(ACIM; Text; Chapter 30; Sec VI; ¶ 1-2)

We are well aware that a number of contemporary self-help books actually ENCOURAGE us to fight. Some authors actually say that those who don't fight, simply do not care about life! These books actually give techniques to fight well. But how about a totally different tactic—making it your goal to give up anger totally? It is so much better for your health and happiness.

Here is a poignant process: Write down this:

"The fear I have of giving up my anger and conflict forever is_____."

Don't say "I don't know," or, "I have given it up." You would probably be walking on water and raising the dead if you had. Just write down what you hear. Many people say they would "not be heard," or they would "feel defenseless." Others would "walk all over them" if they did not maintain their option for anger.

But the fact of the matter is that anger is a defense, and defenses attract more attack. You may not be feeling the anger you have suppressed, but it is there. And it is attracting situations that will "prove it is justified." Until we look at this basic human problem, we will remain unevolved, and unable to ascend. Anger is a block to our spiritual evolution. And as I said before, outbursts of anger can negate the years of spiritual work you have already done on yourself. So, we have to consider giving it up if we wish to ascend into our Self of Unconditional Love.

The best solution for anger that I have ever learned was something taught to me by Babaji.

- ❖ He said you should not suppress your anger; that hurts your body.
- ❖ He said you should also not express your anger; that hurts the other person.
- ❖ The thing to do is to CHANGE THE THOUGHT that causes the anger and breathe out the bad energy.

So, in our relationship what we do is this: If one of us is charged about something, we say: "I am feeling activated. The negative thought that is making me feel activated is_____." That way we are not pretending we are not upset. But we are not indulging in any anger either. Expressing the thought dilutes the anger. If there is a huge charge you can run around the block several times or take a cold shower or get a breathing session. But usually just expressing the thought works.

Comic behavior is another way of keeping an argument from building up or stopping one. Did you know that some police officers are even taught to use comedy to stop a domestic fight? They are taught to end a domestic fight by acting in an unexpected or humorous manner. For instance, they may walk over to the refrigerator and help themselves, making a sandwich. This is a shock to the battling partners, and they often stop fighting!

There are those who find peace boring and believe that life would be very dull without the drama of troubled relationships. We must simply ask these people, "Are you willing to see it differently?" Life without drama is not boring; you get very, very, creative. All we have to do is tune into the spirit of peace. When we do, all the glory of the Kingdom of Heaven opens to us. This joyous experience creates a passion so exhilarating that once you feel it, you will never wish to revert to conflictive behavior again. Also, you get in touch with a higher truth— Peace is Power.

GUILT

Correctable mistakes can be free of guilt if we so choose. Many of us have done things we regretted later. Or we made mistakes we had to correct. But guilt is unnecessary when it comes to correcting a mistake. In fact, guilt is a major mistake that needs to be corrected in our mind if we are to be enlightened and have enlightened relationships.

But what usually happens is we feel bad when we make a mistake. Or we feel angry when someone else does. Or we feel fear when things are thrown off as a result of our mistakes. These feelings then contribute to this corollary feeling of guilt. But what if we decided right now that guilt is always off? Pardon is justified, and correction of errors need not be accompanied by the projection of guilt onto us or others.

This is from Chapter 13 in ACIM, *The Guiltless World:*

> *Those whom you see as guilty become the witnesses to guilt in you, and you will see it there, for it is there until it is undone. Guilt is always in your mind, which has condemned itself. Project it not, for while you do, it cannot be undone. With everyone whom you*

release from guilt great is the joy in Heaven, where the witnesses to your fatherhood rejoice.
(ACIM; Text; Chapter 13; Sec IX; ¶6)

Your only calling here is to devote yourself, with active willingness, to the denial of guilt in all its forms.
(ACIM; Text; Chapter 14; Sec V; ¶3)

Guilt projected onto someone else does not keep us free of guilt. What we give to another we give to ourselves. This is a law. Guilt is an attack on the reality of our Self as God created us. And the part of our "self" that makes mistakes and feels "guilt," or projects it onto others, is not our true Self. Somewhere it says in the Course that God does not forgive because God does not condemn. This is like saying the Self God created did not make the mistake of guilt, therefore it remains innocent all the time. This higher Self does not make errors. The part of us that does is not our higher Self. Forgiveness is merely the process of letting go of this error-ridden self, through giving more attention to our God-created Self.

Guilt, sin, and punishment of death are the errors of the ego. And these are keeping us in a self-imposed "hell" we made up. Isn't it time to accept our original innocence instead of this false religious theology of "original sin?" Isn't this our time to let go of the guilt of our ego in preference to the innocence of our Self as God created us?

Remember this: Every moment you are either choosing the ego's thought system or the Holy Spirit's thought system.

FORGIVENESS

The word means a *cleansing* or *blotting out* of transgression. To forgive means to "give for" to "replace" the ill feeling, to gain a sense of peace and harmony again. To forgive literally means to give up that which you should not have held onto in the first place.

We have a good piece of advice that we give to couples and practice ourselves: "Keep no records of wrongdoing." When a couple commits to this, disagreements are cleaned up right away, in the moment. They go for the highest thought and commit to a *conflict-free* relationship. They value peace above all else. They do not hold grievances from the past, even the immediate past—like five minutes ago.

ACIM says this about forgiveness:

> *The unforgiving mind is full of fear and offers love no room to be itself.*
> *The unforgiving mind is sad without the hope of respite and release from pain.*
> *The unforgiving mind is torn with doubt, confused about itself and all it sees.*
> *The unforgiving mind is afraid to go ahead, afraid to stay.*
> *The unforgiving mind does not believe that giving and receiving are the same.*

> *Forgiveness is the key to happiness. You who want peace can find it only by complete forgiveness. All forgiveness is a gift to yourself. The holiest of all the spots on earth is where an ancient hatred has become a present love.*

> *(ACIM; Workbook; Lesson #121)*

When your good is delayed, that is the time to forgive. This is from Catherine Ponder:

> *If you have a problem, you have something to forgive. Anyone who experiences pain has a need to forgive. Anyone who finds himself in unpleasant circumstances has a need to forgive. Where there is suffering, unhappiness, lack, confusion, or misery of any sort, there is a need to forgive.*

> *Resentment, condemnations, anger, the desire to get even or to see someone punished or hurt, are things that rot your soul and tear*

*down your health. You must forgive injuries and hurts of the past
and present not so much for the other person's sake as for your
own.*

SETTLING ARGUMENTS

Most arguments start when two people have different opinions and each
one asserts that he is right, and the other is wrong. Here is a method to
break that pattern. It is called ***The Highest Spiritual Thought Game:***
1.   Each person drops their "position."
2.   Each person gives up the need to be right.
3.   Each agrees to GO FOR SOLUTION!

Together they look for what would be the highest spiritual thought that
would be the solution. The highest thought is going to be the one that is
the most positive, the most loving, the most productive, and it feels the
best in your body. You keep looking for a higher and higher thought back
and forth and you come up with a thought you both like and agree upon.

It does not matter which of you gets the final high thought. If Markus
gets it, I gladly go up to his thought. If I get it, Markus gladly goes up to
my thought. There is no competition in this.

If you get two thoughts and you cannot tell which is the highest, you take
a break and meditate on that. When such a thought presents itself, you
both have a feeling of joy and relief. A child could even channel the
highest thought.

No records are kept as to who gets the highest thought and how often.
Today, one person may be more open; tomorrow it may be the other.
And while you are at it, make this statement to each other: "I am willing
to keep no records of wrong-doing in my relationship."

I have never seen this game fail when both parties are willing to play it.
The problem is this: The ego is addicted to conflict and sometimes
people forget to play this game. Or they are unwilling to play it because

they want to remain in control and be "right." Well, would you rather have peace or be "right?"

Simple example: How to spend the evening

Let's say your mate wants to go bowling but you want to go to the movies.
What are the possibilities?

1. *Your mate could go bowling with friends and you could go to the movies with friends or alone.*
2. *You could go bowling with your mate and get off your resistance and he or she could go with you to the movies the next night.*
3. *You could do something totally different than either of these— something you both like—stay home and make love!*

Discuss each option together, determining which one would be the most fun and valuable. Keep going until you both win! The Highest Spiritual Thought Game always works when you are willing to play it. When you do, you feel good. When you don't a couple tends to accumulate little differences; these little differences grow into big ones, and then you may find yourself in the 30 years of misery mentioned above in the Hazelton Study.

THE SYMPTOMS OF INNER PEACE

When people are committed to inner peace, they have it. It is a conscious attention paid to living without conflict, grievances, upsets, attacks, dissatisfactions. When these arise, a person committed to inner peace will do everything in their power to undo them in the moment. In this way he or she does not accumulate memories of inner trauma and conflict.

A person committed to inner peace exhibits these *symptoms:*

1. The tendency to think and act spontaneously rather than from fears based on past experiences
2. An unmistakable ability to enjoy each moment
3. A loss of interest in judging one's self
4. A loss of interest in judging others
5. A loss of interest in conflict
6. A loss of interest in interpreting the actions of others
7. A loss of ability to worry
8. Frequent overwhelming episodes of appreciation
9. Contented feelings of connectedness with others and nature
10. Frequent attacks of smiling through the eyes of the heart
11. Increasing susceptibility to love extended by others as well as the urge to extend it
12. An increasing tendency to let things happen rather than make them happen

FAMILY PATTERNS

A pattern is what we call "repetitive unconscious behavior." Patterns are often based on repetitive behaviors in our blood families or reactions to those behaviors. Everyone is subject to these patterns.

When there is a lot of love, that is a lot of energy. This energy pushes up your partner's patterns. We say, "Love brings up anything unlike itself, for the purpose of healing and release." In the Loving Relationships Training, we cover the following fourteen relationship and family patterns:

1. *The tendency to create a partner who is the same personality type as one of our parents*
2. *The tendency to create a partner who treats you the way your parents treated you*
3. *The tendency to copy your parent's relationship to each other*
4. *The tendency to attract and receive disapproval from one's mate due to the parental disapproval syndrome*

5. *The tendency to set up a win-lose relationship of competition due to unresolved sibling rivalry*

6. *The tendency to get even and get revenge at parents by taking it out on one's mate*

7. *The tendency to remain like a helpless child waiting for your mate to take care of you*

8. *The tendency to create struggle in relationships because having it easy and smooth is too unfamiliar and too threatening*

9. *The tendency to take out frustration on innocent family members (the scapegoat pattern)*

10. *The tendency to need to be always right and in control (the control pattern)*

11. *The tendency to channel the mind of the blood family. Mother's mind, father's mind or family mind*

12. *The tendency to set up incestuous triangles because of unresolved sexual energy in the family*

13. *The tendency to punish oneself or get punished due to unresolved guilt*

14. *The tendency to sabotage bliss and happiness*

What does one do about these patterns, you may ask? Most of getting over them requires a few simple steps:

1) *Notice the pattern is there*
2) *Admit you are stuck in it*
3) *Forgive yourself and your family for being stuck in it*
4) *Choose out of the pattern*

Try to stay out of blame and shame. These patterns are very deeply rooted in our subconscious mind and may have been operating for many lifetimes. In some way you could not help but being in the pattern. It composes the family shadow that our spiritual masters tell us we need to overcome. So, everyone has to deal with these shadows.

They have a momentum that is reversible, but you have to be willing to see things differently. When you are a little willing, then you have the help of the Holy Spirit to assist you in your process of liberation from these common family patterns. No personal or family shadow can hide from the light of true forgiveness.

TAKING CARE OF YOUR RELATIONSHIP

What do you do when your body starts acting up or breaking down or gets sore, a pain, a fracture and infection? As you know the wisest course of action is to take care of it right away. What if you still don't pay attention? It may very likely get worse and worse until you have a full-blown disease. If, on the other hand, you are careful to heal each problem as it comes up, you can stay healthy.

Now let's consider your relationship in the same way. If you get perturbed at your mate, or upset with your relationship, but don't deal with the problem right away, things build up. Tension builds up. Your relationship quickly becomes unhealthy. By neglecting to take care of the little things, you accumulate poison in your relationship as you do in your body—and your relationship gets diseased. Left untreated, your relationship grows sicker. By the time you try to get emergency help it might be too late. Separation seems the only way out.

Isn't it quite clear you need to take time to clear even the smallest problem in your relationship? It may sound like work. But what is the alternative? Does processing it have to be work? Not if you know clearing techniques that are fun.

For most of us, our formal education offered no guidance in healing ourselves or our relationships. Instead, we must learn from Infinite Intelligence. The first step is to get out of denial. We know couples who quarrel all the time and they believe that bickering is normal, so they do not change. Let's look at the writing on the wall. Let's identify what is off balance right now and handle it.

A healthy way to keep your relationship alive is to say what you want instead of complaining about what you don't want. Staying in the positive you and your mate can work together to achieve your desires.

BLESSING INSTEAD OF JUDGING

Although blessing instead of judging is an ancient practice, it might be new for you to develop the habit of blessing those you want to judge (like your mate).

The kahunas of Hawaii teach that even mentally criticizing others affects *your body*. It certainly affects your mind. They teach that criticism of the self or of others causes stress and inhibits awareness, memory, and energy flow, making you weaker and more susceptible to illness.
Conversely, The Bible teaches us that someone who is thankful for all things will be made glorious and that attitudes of love, praise, and gratitude fill one with and incomprehensible power of the Spirit. These are called "ascension attitudes."

We may know these ideas but applying them at all times is another story. When someone, like your mate, displays a behavior that is intolerable, we usually don't feel like praising them for it, of course. To break the habit of judging that person, try blessing the situation instead. Support the person in moving through the offensive pattern. Bless them, see them as healed of it, and honor and respect their God Self. This does not mean you are condoning the bad or destructive behavior; but you are approaching the correction without a sense of blame or guilt. This is easier to do if the relationship is already placed in the context of conscious blessing. This is easier to do if you have already decided to have a conflict-free relationship.

Blessing what you want daily and focusing on praise as a habit will create a safe space in your relationship. A sense of peace and relaxation should be the context of any relationship; and this should be re-established daily—telepathically and verbally. If a couple makes a point of focusing on praise as a daily discipline, preferably in a sacred space (such as before an altar) then everything that happens is placed in that context. When that context is repeatedly re-established, each partner becomes more willing to resolve issues and work out his or her own dark shadows with the support and encouragement of the other. If your mate knows, with certainty, that you continually bless him and do not judge his or her true being, then he will not be threatened by discussion of those actions or habits that need to be corrected in order for him to become enlightened.

However, if someone has come from a home where criticism and verbal abuse was common, he may not only expect criticism, but may try to draw that same behavior out of his mate. The mind seeks familiarity. He may unconsciously want criticism and judgment so that he will "feel at home." Or he may want it so he can feel the familiar resentment. Praise and gratitude might even seem suspicious to a mind addicted to criticism. This self-induced pattern is an obstacle that must be overcome. Enlightened couples must be aware of this obstacle and deal with it together.

BLESSING SITUATIONS

Let's say you find yourself in a place you do not like from which there is no escape. You feel like complaining. Instead ask yourself, "What is my good purpose for having created this situation? What can I learn from it?" Then ask yourself, "How can I lift the resonance here?" The answer is to bless the situation as your teacher and to bless it as valuable, even though it may not have met your standard of quality and beauty.

PRAISE SATURATION

Many people have no idea how great they are. Perhaps they have had tons of parental disapproval. They may be starved for acknowledgment. Praise saturation means you acknowledge them verbally in every way you can think of—and you do it sincerely, finding those qualities that are really great and true in that person.

Start out by saying, "Something I really like about you is_____."

COMMUNICATION

Communication is to a relationship what breathing is to living. When lines of communication are not open, the relationship is doomed to failure. We could write a chapter just on this subject it is so important.

General points:

1. You should have no withholds.
2. You can have peaceful discussions. You can even disagree without an upset.
3. Remember that anger provokes separation.
4. Communication ends separation.
5. Always go for the solution.
6. Compassionate communication is this (also called non-violent communication).
   a. What I observe is _____.
   b. The way I feel about it is _____.
   c. What I need and recommend is _____.
7. There is a big difference between complaints and criticisms. Complaint focuses on an event. Criticism attacks a person's character.
8. Avoid harsh startups that begin with attack, blame, or criticism.
9. Always do a soft startup. Share some responsibility on your part first.

There is such a thing as verbal abuse. When a couple does not have good communication habits, they may be falling into some of these verbally abusive patterns. Here are some categories of a form of verbal abuse by Patricia Evens from her book *The Verbally Abusive Relationship:*

1. *WITHOLDING (Keeping to oneself in order to punish the other)*
2. *COUNTERING, CONTRADICTING & INTERUPTING (Insulting the partner's intelligence)*
3. *DISCOUNTING (Devaluing a partner's experience)*
4. *JOKING (Teasing and invalidating through sarcasm)*

5. **BLOCKING OR DIVERTING** (*Changing the subject or making accusations*)
6. **ACCUSING AND BLAMING** (*Charging one's partner with inappropriate behavior*)
7. **JUDGING AND CRITICIZING**
8. **TRIVAILAIZING & DEVALUING** (*Saying or implying that what a partner says or does is insignificant*)
9. **UNDERMINING** (*Attacking a partner's self-esteem*)
10. **THREATENING** (*Intentionally frightening the other*)
11. **NAME CALLING**
12. **FORGETTING** (*Claiming not to remember or getting foggy*)
13. **ORDERING OR COMMANDING** (*Adopting an authoritarian, dominating and disrespectful tone*)
14. **DENIAL** (*Lying about the facts*)
15. **INTERROGATING** (*Delivering a stream of questions in a hostile way*)
16. **SCAPEGOATING** (*Taking out on your mate things you are upset about elsewhere*)
17. **FEELING HURT** (*Being over-sensitive to suggestions that may actually be helpful*)
18. **EMOTIONAL AFFAIR** (*Sharing intimate things with a confidante not your mate*)

It would be good to read this list and see if you or your mate are doing any of these patterns of behavior in your relationship. Ninety percent of cleaning these things up is to own the fact you are doing them. The other ten is catching yourself when you are doing them and choosing out of that pattern, without any extra guilt added onto it.

There is a communication tool we call The 8-Minute Process. This process helps a couple to be heard by the other, without any interruptions, rebuttals, or defenses. It goes something like this:

Go out to a quiet restaurant with soft music (no noisy music) or a quiet place in your home—comfortable and without any interruptions or distractions. The best place would be with a carpet on the floor, like a restaurant in a beautiful hotel, so that it is not noisy.

The person the most upset shares first for eight full minutes, using non-violent communication, avoiding "you" sentences. (Steer clear of statements like, "You did this, and you did that." "You" sentences are blaming. Avoid blaming.) Partner A shares for eight minutes straight. Partner B just listens. The listener must follow these guidelines.

1. Absolutely no interruptions
2. No rolling of the eyes or making faces
3. No rehearsing the rebuttals
4. Must listen 100% present

Then you switch. Partner B talks for eight minutes. The same listening rules apply to Partner A.

After both are heard, then you can have a discussion. The rules of non-violent communication still apply. These go as stated above: 1) What I observe is 2) What I feel is 3) What I suggest or need is. When a couple uses this 8-Minute Process frequently, communication improves and things clear up. In fact, upsets seldom occur when each person in the relationship feels totally heard and considered.

OUR THREE SECRETS

When you have mastered communication, we have a few other things we do to keep our relationship thriving and clear, free of all conflict. Our three big secrets for great relationships are simple:

1. Remove all negativity!
2. Treat your mate always like you would an honored guest.
3. Both of you practice self-analysis of taking 100% responsibility for everything that happens.

For a comprehensive look at relationships in the new paradigm, check out our book, ***Spiritual Intimacy: What You Really Want with a Mate.***

 **#12.**

AN AISLE OF MORE FORGIVENESS

Markus Writes:

Certain spiritual masters come to these earthly planes to impart something important to humanity. In the case of Jesus, He imparted the perfection of forgiveness. Accepting this forgiveness fully in ourselves could be termed the "atonement." He goes so far in His message of A Course in Miracles to say that our sole responsibility in this lifetime is to accept the atonement for ourselves—in other words, to forgive ourselves completely for all past errors, and forgive everyone as well for their past errors. Even if a person wronged us or harmed us, it is important to see there were thoughts in our subconscious mind that attracted that.

A Course in Miracles could almost be called A Course in Forgiveness. Forgiveness is so central to its basic teachings of enlightenment. Many of the lessons in the Workbook, and much of the Text deal with this theme of forgiveness. The first lesson that mentions it is Lesson #121:

Forgiveness is the key to happiness.

How could something this basic be overlooked in our life? Could it be that we have not experienced a profound happiness because we have not fully forgiven ourselves and the world? Later on in PART II of the Workbook, it says this about forgiveness:

> *Forgiveness recognizes what you thought your brother did to you has not occurred. It does not pardon sins and make them real. It sees there was no sin. And in that view are all your sins forgiven. What is sin, except a false idea about God's Son? Forgiveness merely sees its falsity, and therefore lets it go. What then is free to take its place is now the Will of God.*

You are going to ask how Jesus can say something that actually happened, say a person stole something from you, did not occur. This requires a deep answer, and a deep shift in our world view and our personal view.

It is a matter of levels. And a matter of who we think we are. ACIM makes it clear that we are spiritual beings having a physical experience. And that this being cannot be harmed, hurt, or threatened. This is the Self God created. But we have made up an alternative self. This self of our personality, of our bodies, and all of the functional parts we made up to live in this world of the ego, has separated off from our Higher Self of the Spirit. So, when Jesus says: *what you thought your brother did to you has not occurred,* He is speaking of your Higher Self, the only Self that has reality in Truth. Your brother cannot harm or affect this Self in any way. You could even be murdered or crucified, and this Higher Self is unaffected by that. Your body would be gone, that's all, but not your Self. This spiritual identity is immortal. And this is the Self that forgiveness helps us to accept as our own.

Source Energy is always present. We are eternally connected with this Source Energy. Therefore, we have the potential to be always present. One of Jesus's prayers He gives us in ACIM is this:

> *Spirit is in a state of grace forever.*
> *Your reality is only Spirit. Therefore,*
> *You are in a state of grace forever.*

Let us consider that our reality is only Spirit. Yes, we have bodies, languages particular to our upbringing, our own personal and unique histories, and all our conditioning. Can we go beyond all of that to ponder the possibility that we are much more than a finite bundle of limitations? We are in a state of Grace. We are cared for by a force that is in us, but not made by us. We are cared for by Life Force that is on our side, benevolent to our wishes, and wants our well-being to flourish.

Given these facts, what could make us fear? We would have to be identifying with our body, with our self we made up, with our own special interests that are not necessarily consistent with life as a whole. Guilt, anger, fear and unwillingness are the pillars of the ego. Are we working toward freeing our minds from these limitations? Well, forgiveness is the key to happiness because it is the means by which we can be free.

Spirit am I, a Holy Son of God,
Free of all limits, safe and healed and whole,
Free to forgive, and free to save the world.

This is another prayer in ACIM that has irrefutable logic. But first, we have to accept the premises as true. Do we see that our Self-identity is Spirit? This makes us a "Holy Son of God." Right there we may have to undo false religious theology that may have taught us Jesus was the "only Son of God." Our true Self is the Christ in us. This Self has no limits. This Self has accepted the atonement for himself or herself. Complete forgiveness is the doorway to this Self-realization.

Many people come to us with a lot of grievances toward their parents, ex-spouses, and regrets from their past. We help them rise above these and breathe out the past that is no longer here. One exercise we give them we call the *Forgiveness Test.* It goes something like this:

What is your forgiveness level on a scale 0 through 10 (0 is no forgiveness; 5 is half; 10 is complete forgiveness) on your:

Mother: _____
Father: _____
Ex-Partner: _____
Current Partner: _____
Sibling: _____
Self: _____
Other: _____

If you have a charge, or a grievance toward someone, then that means you have not gone to 10 on them. This includes yourself. We are often surprised how low people's scores are, especially on themselves, or on parents or other family members. When people are not at 10, that means they are harboring anger toward that person or incident. It may be suppressed or denied, but it is there. What is not total forgiveness is some form of attack thought—either mild irritation or intense rage. Both prevent complete forgiveness. And unless forgiveness is total, you will be held in some form of mental conflict. And this inner conflict will eventually attract undesirable outcomes.

You who want peace can find it only by complete forgiveness. No learning is acquired by anyone unless he wants to learn it and believes in some way that he needs it.
(ACIM; Text; Chapter 1; Section VI; ¶1)

Forsake not now your brother. For you who are the same will not decide alone nor differently. Either you give each other life or death; either you are each other's savior or his judge, offering him sanctuary or condemnation. This course will be believed entirely or not at all. For it is wholly true or wholly false and cannot be but partially believed. And you will either escape from misery entirely or not at all. Reason will tell you that there is no middle ground where you can pause uncertainly, waiting to choose between the joy of Heaven and the misery of hell. Until you choose Heaven, you are in hell and misery.
(ACIM; Text; Chapter 22; Section 2; ¶7)

What would complete forgiveness look like to you? Would you be willing to do it? We need the Holy Spirit's help in this. I made up a process I call *The Forgiveness Diet.* It was first explained in one of my earlier books, **The Only Diet There Is** (bit.ly/DietRay).

THE FORGIVENESS DIET

The Forgiveness Diet is really simple. I based it on the incident when someone asked Jesus how many times a person should forgive someone. He said, "Seventy times seven." (490 means completion and new growth in numerology.) So, I created *The Forgiveness Diet* in which you can accomplish this. Here is how I do it, starting with yourself first.

- ❖ Take a sheet of paper vertically.
- ❖ Number one side 1-35 in a column on the left.
- ❖ Number the other side 36-70 as you did on the front.
- ❖ Starting at #1, write, "I, (Your Name), forgive myself completely."
- ❖ Write this statement 70 times.
- ❖ Notice what your mind is sharing while you write it.
- ❖ (Notice how this statement purges out negative thoughts you hold about yourself.
- ❖ Do this for seven days (70 X 7)
- ❖ Take the Forgiveness Test again. You should be at 10.
- ❖ If you are not at 10 on yourself, you are unwilling to forgive.
- ❖ If this is the case, write this 108 times in one sitting, "I pray to God, a power greater than myself, for the willingness to change."

You may need to do this Forgiveness Diet a couple of times on yourself if you are stubborn. Most people are stubborn. Unwillingness is very strong in us. We feel self-righteous and feel our grievances and anger are justified. But here is what the spiritual masters say about that:

Anger is never justified. Attack has no foundation. It is here escape from fear begins and will be made complete. Here is the real world given in exchange for dreams of terror. For it is on this forgiveness rests and is but natural. You are not asked to offer pardon where attack is due and would be justified. For that would mean that you forgive a sin by overlooking what is really there. This is not pardon. For it would assume that, by responding in a way which is not justified, your pardon will become the answer to attack that has been made. And thus, is pardon inappropriate, by being granted where it is not due.

Pardon is always justified. It has a sure foundation. You do not forgive the unforgivable, nor overlook a real attack that calls for punishment. Salvation does not lie in being asked to make unnatural responses which are inappropriate to what is real. Instead, it merely asks that you respond appropriately to what is not real by not perceiving what has not occurred. If pardon were unjustified, you would be asked to sacrifice your rights when you return forgiveness for attack. But you are merely asked to see forgiveness as the natural reaction to distress that rests on error, and thus calls for help. Forgiveness is the only sane response. It keeps your rights from being sacrificed.
(ACIM; Text; Chapter 30; Section VI; ¶1-2)

We have to keep reminding ourselves that only loving thoughts and actions are true, and everything else is a cry for help. How will we respond to that call? With anger and non-forgiveness, or with the real help of undoing and absolution? Responding to any form of attack with more attack is being part of the same mistake. True forgiveness is the only way to ascend into the Self God created without slipping back into an ego conflict. And this is always taking 100% responsibility for everything we attract into our frequency of experience.

There is a simple way to find the door to true forgiveness and perceive that it is open wide in welcome. When you feel that you are tempted to accuse someone of sin in any form, do not allow your mind to dwell on what you think he did, for that is self-deception. Ask instead, "Would I accuse myself of doing this"?
(ACIM; Workbook; Lesson #134; ¶9)

Are we willing to ask this question any time we would like to accuse someone of anything less than pure joy and divine perfection: "Would I accuse myself of doing this?" We may have a whole different perspective of them and the situation. We can choose peace instead of what we are seeing in them, and we can rise above our judgments of ourselves which they are just mirroring. This takes daily practice. Forgiveness is the key to happiness, but we have to become masters of it. I will leave you with another thought from Jesus of A Course in Miracles about forgiveness:

The real world is the state of mind in which the only purpose of the world is seen to be forgiveness.

(ACIM; Text; Chapter 30; Sec. V; ¶1)

#13.

AN AISLE FOR SEX

A Course in Miracles would say that all that matters about sex is whether you are in the ego's thought system or you are in the Holy Spirit's thought system with it. If you are in the Holy Spirit's thought system, then it will be a sacred, holy experience. If you are in the ego's thought system, it could be painful in many ways.

As Rajneesh once said: "The primal energy of sex has the reflection of God in it." Sex is Divine. It is the energy that creates new life. Therefore, you should accept sex with joy and acknowledge its sacredness. When a man approaches his woman, he should have a sacred feeling as if he were going to a temple. A woman should be full of the reverence one has for nearing God. Orgasm is for the momentary realization of samadhi. The ego vanishes. In tantric teachings, sexual love represents a sacrament in which the ultimate goal is union with God.

The space a couple choses for lovemaking should be like a temple. We recommend an altar in the room. Make the whole space as lovely as possible. There should be fresh flowers and candles. Television, library books, stacks of stuff, and old bedding are not conducive to holiness. "Prepare the room for God" is always a good practice in creating an atmosphere of the highest vibration for sexual communion.

Sex is a communion of the highest order. Two people come together to share their Divine Connection. The body is lifted to ecstatic heights of innocence and grace. Two people come together to make their will one with God's. The sexual closeness is a Divine closeness. It is an opportunity to practice spiritual intimacy at the body level, using the body as a "communication device" to raise our physical existence to the level of complete innocence—in the atonement. It is a sacred coming together that transcends the body, even though it is grounded in the sensuality of the body.

SEX AND KARMA

There can be a karmic exchange through sexual activity. Sex is not a simple matter of *connect and disconnect*. Some say that the linking resulting from one single sexual activity may last for approximately fourteen months on the higher planes. That means that the karmic link does not dissolve until fourteen months later. So, think about the consequences before you sleep with someone tonight who may have slept with someone else last night. Sleeping with multiple partners can have karmic, as well as bodily consequences.

What you need to do with sexual energy is to consecrate it. To really devote sex to God, sexuality becomes a form of worship that honors the Divine. When we are making love to our partner, we are inviting the goddess or god in them to come forth. Sexual love becomes a source of Divine Energy then. It is an act of celebration. When done in this sacred manner, sexual union becomes a communion of the highest order. Only good karma can come of it. It becomes a spiritual practice of innocence and joy. It confirms a Heaven on Earth that is our birthright to experience.

It would follow that one would not want to have sex with someone who has not handled their fear, anger, or guilt. If you have done the inner work on yourself to clear these mental and emotional demons from your mind, and now you are going to sleep with someone who has not, then the closeness of this act will erase much of the good work you have done on yourself. Having sex with an angry person sets up a momentum that is going in the opposite direction. It makes for an abrupt reversal of your direction, therefore get ready for a potential "train wreck." Do you really want to risk it?

Sexual intimacy is one of the strongest energies you can play with. It is not a casual matter. It is a Sacred Source of Life, and therefore it needs the honoring that comes with life. This is not to say that all sex must be used for procreation, but it does mean that all sex is sacredly joined with the power of Creation. Creatively speaking, what kind of relationship are you using your sexual energy to manifest in this life? If you are not taking it to the highest realms of reverence, insisting upon a sacred space of emotional, physical, and environmental consecration, then you may be accruing karma that you regret later. Then you will have to clean up your relationship with sex like all the other relationship issues we have been discussing.

SEX AND MARRIAGE

Sex is a union, that is for sure. Two people come together to share the Light, and in this case the joys of the body's sensations. It is also an emotional and psychic bond. And at the highest levels, we see it is a spiritual bond. One could easily equate sex with a kind of yoga—a joining not only of two body-mind-spirit persons, but with the greater mind-body-spirit of earthly planes with heavenly planes. Sex is simply a sacrament of the highest order.

This being said, we are coming from our own personal views on sex and marriage that we have formulated over a long life of pondering its purpose and benefits. Although we do not condemn any sexual activity that brings a sense of well-being to those engaged in it, we do not condone sadism, or infliction of pain, or domination over another, or divorcing of sexuality from spirituality. Although we have no judgments about sex outside of marriage, we see the higher purpose of sex is like any other spiritual practice that involves two people in an intimate sharing—its purpose is for the evolution of those two people's souls.

We have committed to Sacred Monogamy—call that monogamous marriage if you prefer. This may not sync with other philosophies out there that promote a more polyamorous approach to sacred sexuality. We have chosen monogamous marriage in the name of our spiritual masters and our Divine Mission, to embody a holy relationship in all areas of our life. Where two become one for life, and the bond is free from all conditioned patterns inherited from family limitations, we place our marriage in the hands of God to evolve and perfect. This is enough for us; in fact, it is everything for us. Freedom is in this one universal joining. Our holy relationship then becomes the diamond body for this larger marriage of our individual selves with our Universal Self.

The Tinder Generation may be a whole different subject. We come from the place of satisfaction and fulfillment right now, so we are not searching in this department. Casual sexual partners would not satisfy us for the mission we have chosen. We are more akin to the traditional values of a monogamous bond than the more multiple and sexually fluid bonds of the new millennium. Divinity could embrace polyamory. But for us, Divinity embraces our monogamy. This bond is whole and one, just like our bond with God is whole and One.

God is in the first place for us, even in our sex life. And we remain open for God's blessings upon the variety of relationships available in the new millennial age. Having said this, we wrote the Second Edition of *I Deserve Love* (bit.ly/DeserveRay) in which a whole section called the Rainbow Millennium is discussed. LBGTQ is simply the new reality of options available, and we embrace people's freedom of choice. But even in this LBGTQ community of choices, our gay and lesbian friends who are happiest are the ones who are in long lasting monogamous holy relationships. They have combined sex and marriage. This is what seems to work best for them as it does for us.

GREAT SEX AFTER SIXTY

Although I never give my age being an immortalist (in the vibe of the ageless), I openly admit I found Markus late in life. I was in my sixties, you might say. And furthermore, he was in his fifties, so there was more than a decade between our ages. But that did not matter in the least bit. We knew we had a Divine Purpose for being together, and this brought us immense joy and satisfaction. We knew our spiritual masters put us together, so you might say we had an arranged marriage. It was awesome then, and still is. We got married officially in Herakhan, Babaji's ashram, on April 4, 2009, after being together more than a year. And this year, 2021, we passed our twelve-year wedding anniversary.

When Markus came to me from Philadelphia, I was living in Marina Del Rey in Los Angeles. He had been studying with his spiritual master, Tara Singh, for 17 years. He also was completing a thirty-year marriage that was his "old life." He brought with him very little baggage— literally and figuratively speaking. He arrived with two suitcases, a few choice books, two leather jackets (one brown and one black), and a set of Henkel kitchen knives. I thought that was funny at the time, but we actually needed the knives. He left everything else, including two properties, and two vehicles, to his ex-wife. We felt so free. Unencumbered by anything. It was wonderful. We would take long walks together and go out on the Marina Del Rey pier, inhaling the ocean air and appreciating the remarkable view—it was so romantic.

Markus and I had many discussions on how we wanted our relationship to be in the beginning. We were looking at this issue of sex in our relationship. He said to me on one of our early morning walks, "I am not too much into celibacy." WOW. Well, when I really looked at the issue myself, I had been single for many years and was focused on my mission. I felt so close to Babaji and the Divine Mother I did not really feel I was missing out by not having a sex-life. But now the game had changed! For the first time I was in a relationship that felt totally aligned with this mission, and how we would define it would be very important. Our relationship would actually be the model for what we were to teach and share with the world. What about sex? We wanted to be conscious about it, so we were clear for others in this major area of life.

After menopause, my sex drive really decreased. I did not feel like I needed it to feel fulfilled. I had other things to do in the mission—getting people to India, to Babaji's feet, spreading the LRT and rebirthing worldwide, writing books, traveling around the world—I was never bored, nor did I ever feel like I was missing out. My life was what it always had been. "More fun per hour." But then Markus came, along with a relationship in the New Paradigm for me—a game changer, to say the least! Immediately our intimacy was in the forefront of my life, and this included sex!! So, I just kept surrendering to this new development. And it was fun.

Our intimacy began with the most important factors already in place. 1) We felt a deep connection from the heart. 2) We agreed to have a "conflict-free" relationship. 3) We engaged in great and honest communication about everything, and we had the means to process ourselves on our issues through Liberation Breathing and other spiritual practices. 4) We put our Spiritual Mission in the first place, and this invoked in us what we now call "spiritual intimacy." 5) We were very loving and patient with one another to discover the best rhythm and joy for sexual pleasure and expression in our new relationship.

At first, I had to get back in the flow after being single for years. But Markus was so sweet and loving on this point. He said, "Let's not make it a problem." And the other thing was for me was the environment. It has to be in the right vibe. Sometimes on the road we are not in a hotel or a person's home that is conducive to sexual intimacy. I have to have everything perfect, in a holy way, and feel the surroundings support our love making. (Perhaps that is just overcompensating for my personal lie, "I'm not perfect.") When I have this right on, I can get in the mood quite easily.

Without getting too explicit about the whole thing, we make love when the environment is just right, especially at home, where we have "prepared every room for God." In India, the lingam and the yoni are honored in a sacred way, so we just transfer this sacred honoring of the male and female principles to our sex-life. We consider all sex acts to be ones of deep and fulfilling sacred worship. This is what sex should be, and this is what it was designed to be by our Creator—an instant

"Nirvana on Earth," based on the orgasmic bliss we were given by God to be one of our greatest human joys.

As I said after menopause my body changed. I did not have the sex-drive I had when I was younger. But again, Markus, said, "Let's not make it a problem, quality is more important than quantity." I was amazed.

The other thing that is important to know, you who are over sixty, there is usually only one speed that works for women in sex at this age, or possibly any age—and this speed is SLOW! Foreplay begins with "taking out the trash," one of my girlfriends once said. So, you have to have the whole day in harmony, and by the time you get around to the actual lovemaking, there is clear space and a feeling of relaxation and beauty. Markus has always been sensitive to my rhythms and accepts my desire for everything to be just right in the timing and the environment.

Foreplay is essential. Building up to penetration is a must. This is why we like oral sex so much. It opens everything up. And then penetration is naturally flowing, and even that has to be slow, in degrees. Play some great music as well. We love classical Indian music during lovemaking. It starts out so slow, and builds in rhythm and intensity, just like the act of lovemaking itself. Light a few candles. Make sure the room is neat, and all other things put away. In order to have great sex you have to have a great environment and atmosphere. What would be a great atmosphere for you? It has to suit both of you. If one partner likes to play rock and roll and the other likes classical music, you might have to work out a deal and play easy jazz. This whole thing is a beautiful dance then, and the results will be that your sex life takes you to the stars.

 # #14.

AN AISLE FOR MONEY

Here are some of the most simple and profound statements I have found about money:

> *You demonstrate success or failure according to your habitual train of thought. Success is a state of mind. Success around money is a state of mind.*

> *You either have a prosperity consciousness or a poverty consciousness. Money responds to which one you have.*

> *Wealth is a state of consciousness. You are at cause of receiving. Only you can deprive yourself of anything.*

> *You can go to the ocean with a teaspoon or a bucket. The ocean does not care.*

> *God does not give you money and houses. God gives you Divine Substance. Substance is the underlying cause, foundation, or creative energy. Substance waits for you to mold it with your thoughts.*

God does not have a problem with you having money as long as it does not control you. You should have money to carry out His purposes.

In the Bible, John 3:2 says: "Beloved, I wish above all things that thou mayest prosper and be in good health."

It is your Father's pleasure to give you His Kingdom.

You must never think for a moment that the supply is limited.

There is nothing wrong with wanting to be rich. The desire for riches is really the desire for a fuller life and that is praiseworthy. The desire for riches is simply the capacity for larger life seeking fulfillment.

There is a science to getting rich:

> *1st You have to believe that there is one intelligent Substance from which all things proceed.*

> *2nd You have to know that this Divine Substance wants to give you everything.*

> *3rd You have to have a relationship with this Divine Substance, and you do that by having deep profound gratitude.*

The mental attitude of gratitude draws the mind into closer touch with the Source. The law of gratitude must be observed. Give thanks continuously. If your gratitude is strong and constant, the reaction of the formless substance will be strong and continuous. Doubt and uncertainty move things away from you. Anger, fear, and guilt prevent the channel from working.

You must have efficient action. Every act you do is either a success or failure. Every inefficient act is a failure. The cause of failure is doing too many things in an inefficient manner. Do each act in an efficient manner. Do them well. Successful action is cumulative in its results. You build a success consciousness. Do one thing well and complete it. These are "little successes." You add up a chain of little successes and this amounts to a bigger success. This is the principle of efficient action.

Fix your attention on the best and surround yourself with the best.

PROSPERITY OF THE SPOKEN WORD

Catherine Ponder would have us say aloud:

Beloved Presence of God. I hereby ask and humbly pray with all my heart and soul and mind for Divine Abundance too be made manifest through my personal fortune and success.

I am willing to move beyond fear in order to fulfill God's plan on earth and beyond. I personally pledge to open myself to financial wealth in order to fulfill my group and individual service commitments.

In God's name, I accept my Divine heritage right now. And thank thee for the timely answer to this prayer. God's will be done.

Invocation for abundance from the I AM Presence:

To the light of God that never fails, I AM the Presence of the Mighty God Power here on earth. I invoke the three rays of Prosperity to be here now: The green ray/ the gold ray/ the violet ray and I know my prosperity is complete.

I am my Beloved I AM Presence invoking the full power of the violet flame to transmute, cause, core, effect, record any memory, every thought, feeling, word or action expressed in any time from or dimension, both known and unknown that reflects poverty consciousness or limitations of any kind.

THE POWER OF GRATITUDE

The very best book we recommend on this subject is *The Path of Wealth* by May McCarthy. She recommends writing a gratitude journal to your CSO (Chief Spiritual Officer). This could be Jesus, Babaji, or the Divine Mother for us. On the left page you write, "Dear CSO, I am so happy and grateful I now have _____." Then list 5-10 things you have that really bring you joy and gratitude.

On the right page you do the same thing, but list things that you have not manifested yet. But treat them as though you already have manifested them. Think about the feelings you will have when these things are in your energy field. You have to realize that God and the masters—your CSOs—really want you to have all your desires fulfilled. But it is your job to keep yourself in the vibration of joy and gratitude no matter what. The power of gratitude attracts not only the good feelings that bring a joyous and fulfilled life, but they keep you in the flow of Divine Grace that gives and gives and never runs out.

Dear CSO, I am so happy and grateful I now have:	Dear CSO, I am so happy and grateful I now have:
1. (Things you already have)	1. (Things you want to manifest)
2.	2.
3.	3.
4.	4.
5.	5.

Gratitude and giving go together like having and extending. The having is acknowledged when it is extended. Gratitude is increased when one gives it away. Acknowledging the gratitude to yourself in a nice journal keeps you in the flow of giving it away. The more you make notes of the blessings in your own life, the easier and more natural it feels to give blessings to others. This is the metaphysical Law: "Today I learn the Law of Love, that what I give my brother, is my gift to me." (ACIM; Lesson #344)

You might ask, how can I say I am happy for something I don't have yet? Well, it's a matter of a vibrational match. If you know God wants you to have all your desires fulfilled, and you are not receiving this fulfillment, then you are stuck in the vibrational match of *unfulfillment*. The purpose of keeping a gratitude journal is to keep you in the vibrational match of *having fulfillment*.

"I am so happy and grateful I now have," is a statement of affirmation, abundance, acknowledgement, and ultimate fulfillment. This is the vibration of receiving. To be in the vibrational match of *not having* just gives us more of *not having*. Thoughts and feelings (which are thoughts manifesting in our inner world) have this power to create joyful results or make unsatisfactory results. Which we choose to focus on will be the decider in any outcome.

The power of gratitude is a mighty power. Life provides an abundance of sustaining elements. There is always enough air. There is an infinite supply of the greater Divine Substance that is not confined to physical stuff. It is also a mental / spiritual stuff. Everything is imbued with Truth, Consciousness, and inner joy or bliss. This transcends the physical senses but can be reached with an inner awareness that does not rely on the senses of the body. The yogic sages, when they meditated on the nature of life, coined the term Sat-Chit-Ananda to describe the ultimate Reality—Truth, Consciousness, Pure Joy. The gratitude connects us with this infinite power. When we are in the vibration of pure joy, our point of attraction for money is increased.

Abundance wishes to flow to areas that are already susceptible to more abundance. Thoughts and feelings of scarcity have a way of blocking the flow of Sat-Chit-Ananda. When our thoughts and feelings are heavy, or blocked, we push money away. If we are angry, we notice life does not flow our way; people do not want to give an angry person their wholehearted support. Hesitation and distrust orbit about an angry person. Fear increases, which further blocks the inflow of manna. By manna I just mean the life-sustaining Divine Substance. Once you have a profound gratitude for this Divine Substance, even if you cannot see, hear, smell, taste, or touch this mysterious matter, then you have a relationship with it. This can be nurtured, and pressed to bear upon matters that include inflow, outflow, and exchange of money.

MARKUS ON SIMPLICITY

Babaji gave us the formula for happiness. Truth, Simplicity, Love and Service to Humanity. These are the four main pillars of His teaching. In them is a call to simplify. When it comes to money, there is a simple rule: only spend within your means for things that enhance and bring joy to your life.

There is money *coming in* and money *going out*. Everyone has these two functions. When money coming in is greater than money going out, there is a favorable balance of trade, and one's resources automatically increase. The means are balanced and in harmony. This is simplicity. When money going out on spending is greater than money coming in, there is imbalance. Debt accrues. Fear can be activated. This is not simple.

Everyone has had times in their life when they have borrowed money or put too much on the credit card. Sometimes these borrowings are necessary. But the idea is to be free of all debts in this life, not only financial, but also psychically and spiritually. The purpose of karma is to be free of karma. Karma is just the cause and effect of something. If one's finances are in a state of debt, there is negative karma. One cannot have something free to give under the duress of debt. So, this would be the first advice if you find yourself in too much debt—begin to seriously pay it off and free yourself of debt. This may seem insurmountable. But you can ask your spiritual masters to help you with this. You need determination on this point.

Credit card usage is very tempting when there is a slowing down of income. But we would need to process your blocks to receiving: it could be your personal lie getting in the way—"I am a failure," I am unworthy," "I am not enough," "I am undeserving," "I am depleted." These are just a few personal lies that could be lodged in your subconscious mind in need of forgiving and clearing. These subconscious thoughts would be putting you in a "poverty consciousness." And your credit card bill could be reflecting this every month.

When it comes to using the credit card, we have a few ground rules: We only use it to the degree we can pay off the bill every month in full. Therefore, it is more of a financial accounting tool. We do not need to write checks or carry much cash. We just use plastic to keep our finances simple. At the end of the month, we pay the balance in full—always. We never leave a balance on the card that would accrue an interest payment. Consequently, we have ZERO interest payment every month. And we get bonus miles for flights from our credit card company.

Our means and ends are kept simple. We maintain a favorable balance of income vs. expense. Therefore, we have no debt. Our "money karma" is clear. We live like a king and queen and don't deny ourselves anything that brings us joy. Our joy is an internal matter. The money we do earn brings us a lot of joy to the degree we give and serve others. And this is from a "selfish perspective." We are selfish in the sense that all our giving blesses us first, and then all people to whom we serve. Sacrifice does not exist in our reality. We give from the Well of our own Divine Abundance. Everyone has this birthright. Coming from simplicity, keeping your means and ends pure, you can create this Wellness Reservoir of Joy too, with all the money you need to do it!

THE PRINCIPLE OF NON-WASTE

Tara Singh was my teacher of A Course in Miracles. He taught me the principle of non-waste. Basically, it adhered to buying only what is essential. But it also had the principle of good quality. Never buy second-hand or calculate below a standard just to "save money." Buy the best, in other words. Never sacrifice quality for frugality.

This applied to clothing, food, and basically everything we would have to enrich our life. He spoke of spending his last dime on classical music albums when he was first living in New York City in the 1950s. He felt the absolute necessity to get to know the highest things in Western culture to get to know the difference between the West and his Eastern roots. To him this was just as much of a need as food, clothing, and shelter. It was food for his soul.

But when it came to a wide range of other things people think they need, they were eliminated from his menu of essential goods. This kind of self-restraint was strong in him. "It takes a religious mind to say no to an indulgence," he would say. But then He spoke of flying to Paris just to get a sweater for his teacher, Mr. Krishnamurti. He would say, "The quality of sweaters in the USA were just not up to those made in Europe." And he wanted to honor his teacher with the best, so he would make the journey out of love for his master just to get him the highest quality. Krishnamurti, who did not receive gifts from his students, would receive them from Tara Singh.

 # #15.

AN AISLE FOR HOLY RELATIONSHIP

In this aisle we will discuss matters involving relationships, and more specifically for those interested in a Holy Relationship. Much of what we offer in this aisle is from our study of A Course in Miracles for 45 years, and what we have learned in our own relationship that we consider holy. This aisle is for couples or anyone who wants to see relationships as an arena for spiritual awakening and evolution.

A COURSE IN MIRACLES ON RELATIONSHIPS

The Course's narrator, Jesus, warns us to avoid separation from our Divine Source, and from our brothers and sisters as well. In fact, He says this is the only problem we have in life to solve: our imagined separation from our Source (God) and from our fellow humans. In appreciating one another, we honor the Holy Spirit most deeply. This applies to couples too—two joined to form one. This is the deal. Separation is healed totally in a holy relationship of this kind.

Here are some passages I really like from ACIM about holy relationships:

> *You cannot understand yourself alone. This is because you have no meaning apart from your rightful place in the Sonship and rightful*

place of the Sonship is God. (ACIM; Text; Chapter 5; Section III; ¶8)

Your gratitude to your brother is the only gift I want. I will bring it to God for you, knowing that to know your brother is to know God. If you are grateful to your brother, you are grateful to God for what He created. Through your gratitude you come to know your brother, and one moment of real recognition makes everyone your brother because each of them is of your Father. (ACIM; Text; Chapter 4; Section VI; ¶7)

The choice to judge rather than to know is the cause of the loss of peace. You have no idea of the tremendous release and deep peace that comes from meeting yourself and your brothers totally without judgment. In the presence of knowledge all judgment is automatically suspended. (ACIM; Text; Chapter 3; Section VI; ¶2)

When you correct a brother, you are telling him that he is wrong. He may be making no sense at the time, and it is certain that, if he is speaking from the ego, he will not be making sense. But your task is to tell him he is right. He is still right because he is a Son of God. If you point out those errors of your brother's ego you must be seeing through yours—because the Holy Spirit does not perceive his errors—nothing the ego makes means anything. When a brother behaves insanely, you can heal him only by perceiving the sanity in him. (ACIM; Text; Chapter 9; Section III; ¶2)

The ego is incapable of trust. It believes that your brothers are out to take God from you. Whenever a brother attacks another, that is what he believes. Projection always sees your wishes in others. If you choose to separate yourself from God, that is what you think others are doing to you. (ACIM; Text; Chapter 7; Section VII; ¶9)

The ego cannot tolerate release from the past. It dictates your reactions to those you meet in the present from a past reference

point, obscuring the present reality. You will then react to your brother as though he were someone else, and this will surely prevent you from recognizing him as he is now. His past has no reality in the present. (ACIM; Text; Chapter 13; Section IV; ¶5)
The Holy Spirit reaches through the body to others. You do not perceive your brothers as the Holy Spirit does. Because You do not regard bodies solely as a means of joining minds and uniting them with yours and mine. If you use the body for attack, it is harmful to you. Communication ends separation. Attack promotes it. (ACIM; Text; Chapter 8; Section VII; ¶2-3)

Remember that those who attack are poor. If you will recognize that all the attack you perceive is in your mind and nowhere else, you will at last have placed its source and where it begins it must end. You have no enemy except yourself. (ACIM; Text; Chapter 12; Section III; ¶3)

Beware of the temptation to perceive yourself unfairly treated. (ACIM; Text; Chapter 26; Section X; ¶4)

When you meet anyone, remember it is a holy encounter. As you see him you will see yourself. As you treat him you will treat yourself. As you think of him, you will think of yourself. Never forget this. Wherever two Sons of God meet they are given another chance at salvation. (ACIM; Text; Chapter 8; Section III; ¶4)

Only appreciation is an appropriate response to your brother. Gratitude is due him for both his loving thoughts and his appeal for help, for both are capable of bringing love into your awareness if you perceive them truly. (ACIM; Text; Chapter 12; Section I; ¶6)

You cannot be hurt, and do not want to show your brother anything except your wholeness. Show him that he cannot hurt you and hold nothing against him, or you hold it against yourself.

This is the meaning of "turning the other cheek." (ACIM; Text; Chapter 5; Section IV; ¶4)

The way to recognize your brother is by recognizing the Holy Spirit in him. The idea of the Holy Spirit is strengthened by being given away. It increases as you give it to your brother. Your brother does not even have to be aware of the Holy Spirit in himself or in you for this miracle to occur. See him through the Holy Spirit in his mind, and you will recognize him in yours. What you acknowledge in your brother you are acknowledging in yourself and what you share you strengthen. (ACIM; Text; Chapter 5; Section III; ¶1-3)

The Bible says that you should go with a brother twice as far as he asks. It certainly does not suggest that you set him back on his journey. Devotion to a brother cannot set you back either. It can lead only to mutual progress. The result of genuine devotion is inspiration, a word which properly understood is the opposite of fatigue. (ACIM; Text; Chapter 4; Intro; ¶1)

It is impossible to overestimate your brother's value. It will be given you to see your brother's worth when all you want for him is peace. And what you want for him you will receive. (ACIM; Text; Chapter 20; Section V; ¶3)

THE END OF A RELATIONSHIP

There are times when a relationship has run its course. There is nothing that says a relationship has to be maintained after it is no longer providing the joy that a true holy relationship is meant to supply. If your mutual love for each other is not apparent, then it is best to consider moving on. Staying in a dysfunctional relationship out of fear of leaving will keep you stuck in misery.

If someone leaves, or you leave, your partner is no longer best for you. Nothing is taken from you without it being replaced by something better. If you remember these truths, the disappointments won't hit as hard. If you release the thought "There is nobody else out there," it will be easier. You cannot receive the great good that is coming until you let go of your attachments. Remember the failure of your relationship may actually be to your benefit. Failures can be gains not recognized. No matter what the result of your relationship is, you wanted that result. You created it. You may not be consciously aware of it, but you are always getting what you want. Because you wanted that result, you are a success even if it looked like a failure.

In our work, people sometimes want us to tell them whether they should leave or stay in a relationship. We are very careful not to advise them one way or another. What we can do is help them get clear. We would probably say this: "If you had no fear, no guilt, and you did not care what anyone said, and you knew you could create a new relationship, would you leave or stay in this relationship?" If they say, "I'd then leave," but they are still staying, then they then are out of integrity for staying. And this inner conflict will make their life a misery.

Staying in a relationship that you secretly know is over, just because you are afraid of being alone, is neither kind nor virtuous. It is unfair to you and your mate.

Perhaps you need a Liberation Breathing session to help you with this transition. When a relationship ends, it is important to purify oneself and reflect. This will help avoid making the very same mistakes the next time around. What do we mean by "purify oneself?" It is important to take 100% responsibility for the breakdown. What was in you that you attracted a relationship that was unsatisfying, or even abusive?

Some people feel their separation or divorce was so traumatic that they are afraid to try again. A lot of people are so afraid to get *hurt again* that they don't even try to have a new relationship. This is unfortunate. These thoughts will cause you to be stuck alone. You can do better the next time if you process, "Why I created being hurt," and what thoughts you had that caused that hurt to come to you. If you truly have understood and forgiven yourself, then you will not attract the same kind of relationship again.

Once I had a relationship end and I was feeling very shook up about it. I was going to India after that. When I got to India I was commiserating about the breakup while walking in the park in New Delhi. I literally heard a voice in the air say, "What if leaving could be a joy?" I started arguing with the voice in my mind, and replied, "THAT IS RIDICULOUS." Babaji then said, "Just wait till you see what I have for you next." Lo and behold, He gave me such a wonderful new life beyond the imaginable that I ended up glad that relationship ended.

The main point is not to judge yourself if a relationship ends. Also, let go of all bitterness. This will help you be resilient and allow something better to happen. If you cannot seem to let go and you feel stuck, get some support like a Liberation breathing session.

THE IMMORTAL COUPLE AS A NEW PARADIGM

Instead of getting old together and dying, imagine the opposite. What if both of you could become ageless as a couple and live together as long as you wanted—even hundreds of years! Sounds farfetched? Not anymore. We now have the knowledge to make this happen.

An immortal is a soul who has already experienced enough female and male incarnations that the birth/death cycle can now be transcended. This soul can stay here to serve as long as he chooses. In order for a couple to become immortal together, they have to work out their "unconscious death urge." This is an incredible project for a couple to have. What this does for a relationship is simply incredible. The relationship takes on a whole new vibration of sheer vitality. The sacredness increases also because life is God, and so, more life equals more holiness. When two immortals are together, there is a sense of well-being that pervades the underlying structure of the relationship.

Of course, many people cannot tolerate the idea of physical immortality because it is too exciting! They might be addicted to pain and struggle. Others simply don't want to live forever in a physical body because they hate their life.

When a couple strives for this expression of the Divine, they become strong and healthy, there is a miraculous and free flow of psychic energy. This energy can be channeled into meaningful self-expression. When a couple expresses together the glory of immortality into their life and society, they function as effective instruments for creative action and a realization of higher values in the world. They truly discover what life is at its best!

This is from Lesson #163 in A Course in Miracles:

> *It is impossible to worship death in any form, and still select a few you would not cherish and would yet avoid, while still believing in the rest. For death is total. Either all things die, or else they live and cannot die. No compromise is possible. For here again we see an obvious position, which we must accept if we be sane; what contradicts one thought entirely cannot be true, unless its opposite is proven false.*
>
> *The idea of the death of God is so preposterous that even the insane have difficulty in believing it. For it implies that God was once alive and somehow perished; killed, apparently, by those who did not want Him to survive. Their stronger will could triumph over His, and so eternal life gave way to death. And with the Father died the Son as well.*
>
> *Death's worshippers may be afraid. And yet, can thoughts like these be fearful? If they saw that it is only this which they believe, they would be instantly released. And you will show them this today. There is no death, and we renounce it now in every form, for their salvation and our own as well. God made not death. Whatever form it takes must therefore be illusion. This the stand*

we take today. And it is given us to look past death and see the life beyond. (ACIM; Workbook; Lesson #163; ¶6-8)

A Course in Miracles assures us there is no death. It also assures us our identity as a Son or Daughter of God. From a mental point of view, we can identify with the Spirit or with the ego that thinks it is caught in a body. So how we direct our thoughts is very important. The unlimited nature of Spirit, created by our infinitely Loving Source, is our true Self-identity. But we have free will to identify with limitations—with death, time, and problems. Through a process of redirecting our minds we can forgive ourselves for all our mistakes. We can give up all our fear, guilt, and anger and empty our mind to receive the lofty thoughts of God. In this way we join our mind with the Mind of God and think joyful and holy thoughts. This is the inner work everyone has to do to evolve, and any couple must embrace to make their relationship holy.

Lesson 163 ends on this beautiful prayer:

Our Father, bless our eyes today. We are Your messengers, and we would look upon the glorious reflection of Your Love which shines in everything. We live and move in You alone. We are not separate from Your eternal life. There is no death, for death is not Your Will. And we abide where You have placed us, in the life we share with You and with all living things, to be like You and part of You forever. We accept Your Thoughts as ours, and our will is one with Yours eternally. Amen.

There is no death, for death is not God's Will. Two people in a Holy Relationship align their will with God's, and in so doing conquer death itself.

#16.

AN AISLE FOR DIVINE SERVICE

The reason human beings don't have self-illumination and continuous joy is because of their samskaras, or the accumulated imprints of past experience. Samskaras should be entirely removed for total liberation. It is important to understand the law of karma (i.e., you reap what you sow, what you do to another is also done to you).

Traditionally great beings remove samskaras by renunciation, solitude, fasting, penance, and by desiring nothing. However, living the life of a complete ascetic can be counterproductive to having a relationship. The masters say that you can begin to alleviate conflict by replacing lower values with higher ones. Also, it is recommended that you sublimate your energy into spiritual channels through meditation, devotion, and selfless service.

Our master, Babaji, encourages us to live a life of Truth, Simplicity, Love, Service to humanity; and karma yoga (work dedicated to God and humanity). He told us that karma yoga is the highest yoga and that it can change our fate. He told us that idleness is death. Work is worship. Dedicate all of your work to God every single day. This will change your life for the better. Karma yoga is the yoga of selfless service. It is the path for achieving union with the Divine by shifting our awareness from self-preoccupation to that of serving the needs of others. To practice karma yoga, you don't necessarily have to change what you are doing. You are among the minsters of God already, ACIM says.

Who is your ministry? Everyone who you work with. Everyone in your Facebook friends, email list, and everyone who comes to you during the day. You serve them by helping them raise the quality of their thoughts and by telling them what is available for their healing. These people are not in your life by accident. They are there to aid you in your ascension process.

Karma yoga purifies our heart and prepares us for reception of Divine Light. It helps us attain the knowledge of God. It helps clear us of past-life karma. It helps liberate us from the cycle of bondage to worn out beliefs, memories, and thoughts. It literally frees us from the past.

The only danger of dedicating your life to serving society (such as charity work) is having a false motive. If done for recognition, pride, or for making someone obligated to you, you can do harm to others and yourself by creating more samskaras. Selfless service means that you are willing to give up personal motives. It is also necessary to have a spiritual understanding. For example, you might decide to feed the poor. This can be wonderful. However, a beggar of food might be creating his own samskaras and you may be inadvertently binding him tighter to his pattern. Meeting his basic need for food may be good yet cultivating his mind and raising his self-esteem (so he can return to support himself) is more helpful. This is probably contrary to his pattern. In other words, some service can be disservice if you are not careful.

Serving a sick person's bodily needs and helping them get back on their feet is a valuable service. Anything that you can do to uplift and advance humanity is good service. Remember, it should always come from an outpouring of your being. It should come from a motiveless place in yourself. One in which your giving-ness is bursting from its seams, and you cannot help but to give from the core of your own goodness and Divine Strength.

When I joined the Peace Corps with my first husband back in 1963, after Kennedy's famous inauguration speech about finding what you have to give to your country, we were touched more deeply by this experience than anything else in our lives. I considered that time to be my "boot camp for world service." I was happier than any other time in my marriage because we had nothing but our love and the purest kind of work—service to humanity.

Loving and serving our Earth expands our heart. There is a sheer joy to making a difference. There is nothing that gives back to us more than service. We learn the generosity of giving by serving. Service is not something we do when we have time to do it. It is the wellspring of our being. In regard to this pandemic, we have to face this world crisis and not hide from it. The true meaning of our life is to find a mission to do something about this crisis.

Imagine what would happen if a couple sat down and decided, right from the beginning, what kind of mission they were going to accomplish together for the world and then they actually did it! This spiritual mission could be a joint career such as we ourselves have. If you are already in different careers, you can still decide what kind of service you can offer together. When people are deeply in love, they feel a natural concern for the state of the world, and they want to do something about it. If love has waned and the relationship is stale, it might just be because the couple never acted on that sense of purpose. It is never ever too late to infuse your marriage or relationship with this gift. It is not only a gift to the world, but a gift to the relationship. It gives the relationship true meaning. Everyone is looking for meaning. It is good to focus on something greater than oneself. Missions are satisfying. Big stretches make you expand and at the same time they heal you.

Our prayer is that the material in this book will help you give meaning to your life.

MARKUS ON HAVING A DIVINE MISSION

A purpose-driven life has a cause for dedication. Some people may have a cause to increase their wealth and think solely about their own accumulation of money. Their goals could be confined to their own material success. Yet we have found this kind of cause may be very limited without some mission of service or considering a cause greater than one's own self-interests. There is nothing wrong with accumulating wealth—but to what end? To what cause will your wealth be applied?

We have dedicated our life to the cause of awakening people to their Divine Connection. We have a responsibility then, to place our own Divine Connection at the center of our purpose here, our cause. We have to be in this close Intimacy with our Creator for us to transfer this intimacy to others. We teach what we need to learn, but we have to be certain this Divine Connection is what we are embracing wholeheartedly.

Our Divine Mission is in awakening others to their Self-identity through Liberation Breathing, Spiritual Quests, mental processing, and daily immersion into high-minded philosophies and practices. We use our money to these ends. We help others live more in the frequency of joy. In doing this we put ourselves in more joy. Our Divine Mission is to stretch people's minds to see that even aging and death is a function of thoughts and habits. We use our money to examine all of this, to present seminars that question our beliefs, and to raise our thoughts to the highest possibilities known to us. This Mission gives our money purpose, and keeps it flowing in our storehouse of Divine Providence. What is your Divine Mission? You might like to think about this.

 **#17.**

AN AISLE FOR SOCIAL MEDIA

MARKUS ON SOCIAL MEDIA

We are blessed in this age to have so many channels of communication open to us. Never before have people had so much *power* in their hands to make their thoughts known. And pictures too. Videos, stories, tidbits of brain bites, you name it. It's overwhelming. The ascendency of the internet in the past 30 years has eclipsed the available channels up until that point in history to publish what you want to say. The social media is influential as governments, bigger than any publisher, more at your fingertips than any other public communication medium known to humankind. On the bright side, what gratitude we have for this unlimited facility!

Much of what is posted on social media is silly and sentimental, but for the most part it is a revolutionary medium. We have a responsibility to lift up our message with this medium of unprecedented fluency. Sondra and I endeavor to speak, write, and act from something meaningful, thus we wrote this book: *The Supermarket for a Meaningful Life.* By now you have probably gleaned a few things that will enrich your life for the better and be some of the content you may share across your platforms.

Concerning the social media argument, it can be a tool in the hands of those who endeavor toward the Love and Wisdom of the Ages. In this great sequester we have used the internet in place of our real-time, live workshops and travels as well as the movie theater or television. We have scoured the internet, Amazon, Netflix, and You Tube channels to live stream the best of what education has to offer—from Ken Burns and David Attenborough documentaries to Krishnamurti, Esther Hicks, Joel Osteen lectures, and the latest voices of spirituality of the day. We have used our Facebook, Twitter, and Instagram to keep up with the real time happenings in many different fields of interest, including putting forth our own work. Sondra's last two books—*Lately I've Been Thinking I & II* were filled with four years of her Facebook posts. All these "posts for an awesome life" were tidbits of wisdom from her perspective, shared on a daily basis. We have used ZOOM to teach our workshops on relationships and give Liberation Breathing sessions to our students and clients. Our world has been opened world-wide through these various tools for communication.

Social media is our modern way of communicating, and this medium is interwoven into what is communicated. Meaning is still our responsibility. We try to put out something meaningful and inspiring to our readers and followers. We post frequently, without being merely self-promotional. Marshall McLuhan coined the famous phrase in the early 1960s, when television was coming into its ascendency: "The medium is the message."

> *McLuhan uses the term 'message' to signify content and character. The content of the medium is a message that can be easily grasped, and the character of the medium is another message which can be easily overlooked. McLuhan says "Indeed, it is only too typical that the 'content' of any medium blinds us to the character of the medium." For McLuhan, it was the medium itself that shaped and controlled "the scale and form of human association and action." Taking the movie as an example, he argued that the way this medium played with conceptions of speed and time transformed "the world of sequence and connections into the world of creative configuration and structure." Therefore, the message of the movie medium is this transition from "lineal connections" to "configurations." Extending the argument for understanding the medium as the message itself, he proposed that*

the "content of any medium is always another medium" – thus, speech is the content of writing, writing is the content of print, and print itself is the content of the telegraph.

What is the message of social media? We are all connected. We all have a voice to speak out our truth, be it the repetitions of our own personal preferences, the next sunset we see, the next family gathering, the next funny pet video cascading down our newsfeed, or our new tattoo. But we also have the potential to have deep connection with others about the matters that concern us. It is a place where serious communications can happen if that is our goal.

Social media has become a way of life. One can almost not live without it. Certainly, one can barely live without internet and mobile service. Our heads seem to be more in our devices than in pondering the stars—or our Self as God created us. Can these higher subjects be enhanced by our willingness to ascend? What is the message of social media? Marshall McLuhan's question is still relevant sixty years after he began to pose these questions of relevance, and how the medium of communication is affecting that relevance.

I am typing these words on a MAC, not setting them letter by letter with lead type as Whitman did in the 1850s or pressing cuneiform wedges in wet clay in Mesopotamia to describe the movements of the gods or list the accounts of the next shipment of summer grains. The written word has been a medium for communicating for over 5,500 years.

The general consensus is that Sumerian was the first written language, developed in southern Mesopotamia around 3400 or 3500 BCE. At first, the Sumerians would make small tokens out of clay representing goods they were trading. Later, they began to write these symbols on clay tablets. This earliest form of the language was Sumerian cuneiform, which consisted of "wedge-shaped" glyphs. (https://www.babbel.com/en/magazine/what-is-oldest-word-in-world)

Hark, the herald of literary angels sing—through the wedge-like sticks pressed into the clay of the first social media on a dry plain in southern Iraq, circa 3500 BCE, or through the lead glyphs set by a printing house in the 1850s to make the first copies of Whitman's *Leaves of Grass* known to the world. How far we have come with not only the technology, but with the whole concept of communication—including videos, pictures, words, and documented deeds blasted out to the world in a millisecond. We now have the greatest means of the written word since 1450 and the very invention Guttenberg's printing press and movable type.

Social media is here to stay. What we say with it is up to us. Will we uplift those like Whitman did with our egalitarian words and deeds of inclusion? What inspires us? What news is fit to print from the happenings in our hearts? If the social media upholds real Love in this publicly persuasive organ of expression, the more power to it. Put that love into your next post. Only that has meaning. Only that is the real-time message of words to pictures to videos in this media that is so scintillatingly also the "message."

Social media is our blessing and our challenge. How can we use it to uplift and enhance, to truly evolve the human race and not merely entertain it? For those of us interested in literature, there are quality blog sites that broaden our awareness. *Brain Pickings* by Maria Popova writes weekly one of the best literary blogs in the country: https://www.brainpickings.org/.

If you are into poetry like I am, the *Poetry Foundation* sends out daily posts with the work of new poets: https://www.poetryfoundation.org/. And for longer literary works, the *Library of America* is very good to send excerpts of longer works out weekly: https://storyoftheweek.loa.org/.

You can join our mailing list by going to www.sondraray.com and give your name and e-mail.

Sondra and I have four main Facebook destinations:
https://www.facebook.com/sondra.ray.90
https://www.facebook.com/markus.ray.169

https://www.facebook.com/LiberationBreathing
https://www.facebook.com/SondraRayBooks

We have two Twitter pages:
https://twitter.com/SondraRay1008
https://twitter.com/MarkusRay1008

Here are our Instagram accounts:
https://www.instagram.com/sondraray/
https://www.instagram.com/markusray1008/

We have a Tumblr account as well:
https://immortalray.tumblr.com/

YouTubes are here:
https://www.youtube.com/user/SondraRay
https://www.youtube.com/MarkusRay

We have a Podcast on Relationships here:
https://bit.ly/RayPodcast

We have a Podcast on A Course in Miracles here:
https://bit.ly/PodcastACIM

Sondra's many articles on Relationships are found here:
https://sondraray.com/spirit-pantry

My many articles on Art are found here:
https://markusray.com/art-look/

These links are a Supermarket in themselves. We invite you to do some of your shopping for meaning on these sites. On Sondra's website are many articles on relationships. On my website there are many articles on art. Perhaps you will also join us for one of our online events. Look them over here: **https://sondraray.com/programs-seminars/**

Our Facebook Page

LATELY I'VE BEEN THINKING I & II

Facebook has been a grand platform for us to keep people informed of what we are thinking, about all kinds of things. We write on our Facebook every day, and people receive small doses of important principles, either from our books or from those authors we admire; or simply what is on our mind in the moment.

Sondra's past two books have been compilations of her Facebook posts, all in one place. *Lately I've Been Thinking I* are posts from 2015-2017; *Lately I've Been thinking II* are posts from 2017-2018. As we are in an age of *attention deficit disorder*, people seem most content reading one page or less. This is a perfect literary form to present tidbits of wisdom that are short and sweet—ponderable in one brief sitting. This has been one way social media has affected the style of our writing.

Bit.ly/LatelyRay and *Bit.ly/Lately2Ray*

#18.

AN AISLE FOR THE PURPOSE OF LIFE

The painter Gauguin was in the last few years of his life in French Polynesia when he painted one of his greatest masterpieces. He titled it "Where do we come from? What are we? Where are we going?" Already he had explored the edges of rebellion and left behind a conventional life in Europe. Already his early childhood in Peru among the indigenous folks had developed his affinity for so called "primitive cultures." He was in love with the "noble savage," and in fact he saw the real "savages" in the colonial Europeans who had run roughshod over the globe subjugating the local people. He painted the Polynesians in their colorful element. In fact, these kinds of colors had not likely ever been painted before in the history of European art.

Gauguin had a purpose in life to capture a different kind of beauty. He was not concerned with the approval of the schools of painting that had grown up in Paris and the cutting edge of Western Painting. He used the medium that was age old—oil on canvas—but he took the "message" to a whole new and provocative level. He was questioning the very purpose of life itself.

"Where do we come from? What are we? Where are we going?"

1897; Oil on Canvas; 55" Height X 148" Width
Paul Gauguin; Boston Museum of Fine Arts

This is Gauguin's largest work. Nearly thirteen feet wide. He does not apologize for the lack of "civilized" signposts in the painting. In fact, there are none of the *Western version*. Not a stick of European architecture or influence. The symmetrical God/Goddess about one-fourth of the way in from the upper left is the only "man-made" object in the entire picture. He/She stands on a circular pedestal with raised hands to the sides, seemingly in a kind of mudra or hand position indicating a focus of energy. There is a stillness in this figure—a kind of refreshing neutrality that is almost androgynous. Gazing straight forward without a flinch, not asking us to pay homage, bow down, or otherwise worship. This is the

summation of Gauguin's view on religion: even with a "deity of worship," we still have to figure out our purpose here. "Where do we come from? What are we? Where are we going?" These questions are written in French in the uppermost corner to the left. They are questions written in the heart.

The central figure is imposing. A pillar of verticality, reaching upward; is this character a he or a she? Probably he is picking a ripe fruit. But the figure is clearly looking heavenward. The question of purpose looks to heaven for answers. Various figures are sitting pondering—relaxed but pensive. What is it they ponder? The young girl sitting in the extreme foreground just left of center with two cats is eating a piece of fruit. Behind her is a goat. Two women to the right flank a baby lying by itself asleep. Two friends walk together to the right of center in a tete-a-tete, conversing about something intimate. A black dog comes shooting into the picture plane from the extreme right edge, in a springing gesture. An old woman sits with a duck in the lower left corner. All seem to be asking the question, "Why am I here? What is my purpose." This is the basic question of Life. Gauguin presents it in all its oceanic glory, using so called "primitives." What contribution will we make with our life? What is our purpose here? A Course in Miracles makes it very clear what our purpose is:

Your purpose is to see the world through your own holiness. Thus are you and the world blessed together. No one loses; nothing is taken away from anyone; everyone gains through your holy vision. It signifies the end of sacrifice because it offers everyone his full due. And he is entitled to everything because it is his birthright as a Son of God. (ACIM; Workbook; Lesson #37; ¶1)

Did you ever think your purpose here on earth was to have a holy vision, and to bless the world with this holiness that abides in you?

Certainly, this is what Gauguin was doing in the painting above. He was seeing the humanity of the people in their harmony with nature, amid the Great Questions of Life. By painting them in their innocent glory he was seeing them with Christ's vision—essentially, he was blessing them.

We could say our purpose is to "do something" in the world. Many intelligent people pursue a profession and spend their whole life engaged in their area of expertise. They identify with their career, and this is all okay. But is there something that the profession cannot give in terms of our purpose? Consider these statements:

God is the only goal I have today.
(ACIM; Workbook; Lesson #156)

Let me remember what my purpose is.
(ACIM; Workbook; Lesson #157)

Let me remember that my goal is God.
(ACIM; Workbook; Lesson #158)

They may put your ego into a tailspin because you have been thinking about external goals and purposes. This purpose is God realization, and this is your only purpose here, according to Jesus of ACIM.

The Supermarket for a Meaningful Life would have to contain this Aisle for a Divine Awareness as our Purpose. It can be had in the simplest of observations, in how we pour a cup of coffee for our mate. It could be in the words we use to communicate to our colleagues at our job. It would be how we dress ourselves in the morning.

May this book fill your Spirit Pantry with the food you need to come into this new era. We have survived Covid-19 and the world pandemic. Now it is our purpose to ask the Great Questions:

Where do we come from? What are we? Where are we going?"

And only you can answer these great questions of purpose that is posed to you. May the goodness of Truth, Simplicity, Love and Service found in the aisles of this Supermarket we offer suffice to meet all your needs with Infinite Grace—and then some.

CHECK OUT

Now that you have filled your cart, it's time to "check out." Normally this means you pay for what you put in your cart. But in this case, we don't accept any payment other than what you paid for this book. What we really want you to pay at checkout is to apply the principles we discussed in these aisles to increase your joy, improve your relationships, and enrich your abundance. Also, we would love to hear from you. We would like to know how applying the things you picked up in the aisles of The Supermarket has transformed your life. You can write to us here: immortalrayproductions@gmail.com. We look forward to hearing your stories.

Love,

Washington DC
July 4, 2021

Sondra Ray

Markus Ray

ABOUT THE AUTHORS

SONDRA RAY, author of 29 books on the subjects of relationships, healing, and spiritual matters, was launched into international acclaim in the 1970s as one of the pioneers, along with Leonard Orr, of the Rebirthing / Breathwork experience. She has trained thousands of people all over the world in this conscious connected breathing process and is considered one of the foremost experts on how birth trauma affects one's body, mind, relationships, career, and life. As she puts it, "This dynamic breathing process produces extraordinary healing results in all your relationships—with your mate, with yourself, and with Life— very fast. By taking in more Life Force through the breath, limiting thoughts and memories, which are the cause of all problems and disease, come to the surface of the mind so they can be 'breathed out', forgiven, and released."

Applying over 45 years of metaphysical study, she has helped thousands of people heal their negative thoughts and beliefs, birth trauma, habitual family patterns, and unconscious death urge which affected their life. She encourages people to make lasting positive changes through Liberation Breathing® to be more free, happy, and productive. No matter what Sondra Ray is doing, she is always trying to bring about a higher consciousness. Recently she has written two new books that are tidbits of wisdom she posted on Facebook for over four years: *Lately I've Been Thinking©* and *Lately I've Been Thinking II*. These give any reader a broad overview of her "comments on the road" and her impressions of timeless wisdom she posts daily to her followers.

MARKUS RAY, artist, poet, and twin flame of Sondra Ray, received his training in the arts, holding degrees from the Cleveland Institute of Art and Tyler School of Art of Temple University in Philadelphia. He is the author of a major work, ***Odes to the Divine Mother***, which contains 365 prose poems in praise of the Divine Feminine Energy. Along with the Odes are his paintings and images of the Divine Mother created around the world in his mission with Sondra Ray.

Markus is a presenter of the profound modern psychological/spiritual scripture, **A Course in Miracles**. He studied with his master, Tara Singh, for 17 years, in order to experience its truth directly. His spiritual quest has taken him to India many times with Tara Singh and Sondra Ray, where Muniraj, Babaji's foremost disciple, gave him the name Man Mohan, "The Poet who steals the hearts of the people". In all his paintings, writings, and lectures, Markus creates a quiet atmosphere of peace and clarity that is an invitation to go deeper into the realms of inner stillness, silence, and beauty. He teaches, writes, and paints alongside of Sondra Ray, and many have been touched by their demonstration of a holy relationship in action. His iconic paintings of the masters can be viewed on markusray.com which he often creates while his twin flame, Sondra Ray, is lecturing in seminars.

SONDRA RAY'S Author's Portal :

Bit.ly/SondraRay

MARKUS RAY'S Author's Portal :

Bit.ly/MarkusRay

RESOURCES

Sondra Ray /– Author, Teacher, Rebirther, creator of the Loving Relationships Training®, Co-founder of Liberation Breathing®

- ❖ **Facebook:** www.facebook.com/sondra.ray.90
- ❖ **Facebook Fan Page:** www.facebook.com/LiberationBreathing
- ❖ **Twitter:** www.twitter.com/SondraRay1008
- ❖ **YouTube:** www.youtube.com/SondraRay
- ❖ **Instagram:** www.instagram.com/SondraRay
- ❖ **Website:** www.sondraray.com

Markus Ray /– Poet, author, artist, Rebirther, presenter of A Course in Miracles, co-founder of Liberation Breathing®,

- ❖ **Facebook:** www.facebook.com/markus.ray.169
- ❖ **Facebook Fan Page:** www.facebook.com/LiberationBreathing
- ❖ **Twitter:** www.twitter.com/MarkusRay1008
- ❖ **YouTube:** www.youtube.com/MarkusRay
- ❖ **Instagram:** www.instagram.com/MarkusRay1008
- ❖ **Website:** www.markusray.com/
- ❖ **"Art Look" – an art lover's companion**: www.markusray.com/art-look

301 Tingey Street, SE, #338, Washington D.C. 20003

E-mail: contact@sondraray.com
E-mail: contact@markusray.com
Babaji and The Divine Mother Resources:

Babaji's Ashram in Haidakhan (India)
E-mail: info@haidakhanbabaji.com

We encourage you, our reader, to attend The Loving Relationships
Training (LRT) which is produced by Immortal Ray Productions all
over the world. You can see Sondra Ray & Markus Ray's worldwide
teaching schedule on **www.sondraray.com/programs-seminars/**

Also, we encourage you to attend The INDIA QUEST, The BALI QUEST,
or other Spiritual Quests that teach and disseminate Liberation
Breathing practices, and principles of A Course in Miracles, as well as
enhance your Divine Connection to various spiritual masters. These are
also available on **www.sondraray.com**

Artwork and paintings of the spiritual masters by Markus Ray are
available on **www.markusray.com**

Liberation Breathing   Book a Session at bit.ly/LBSession

IMMORTAL RAY PRODUCTIONS

We at Immortal Ray Productions wish for you to get the most out of your life. Like Henry David Thoreau, we want you to "walk to the tune of a different drummer" and follow your inspirations to the ends of the earth. We help you make this possible. We hope you will join us on one of our Quests—to India, Bali, Glastonbury, Hawaii, Iceland, and new places unexplored—so you will not miss your calling, but rather live your life deliberately and fully, and not wake up one day to discover you had not really lived.

RETURN TO THE DIVINE MOTHER IN BALI, THE ISLAND OF THE GODS, AND THE WORSHIP OF THE SACRED FEMININE !

Join SONDRA RAY on her BALI QUEST , an exquisite journey of the soul to this ancient holy culture.

BALI
QUEST with SONDRA RAY

ARRIVE: DEC 3
DEPART: DEC 13
EVERY YEAR

◆ **JOIN SONDRA RAY** in this life changing event. Journey to **BALI,** one of the most special places on the planet. Discover your sacred Self at most holy **Besakih Mother Temple.**

◆ Pay homage to the Divine Mother of all LIFE in BALI, and usher in 2019 at one of the

"Immortality Power Points". Stretch your mind and open your heart on this profound journey. Visit the sacred waters of **Pura Tirta Empul Temple.**

◆ Arrive in Bali on DEC 3rd and meet the "Mother of Rebirthing", **SONDRA RAY,** to begin this quest of spiritual awakening through **Liberation Breathing®** from the Divine Mother. Witness **Gamelan Music & Balinese Dancing.** Soak up the rich Balinese culture that for centuries has worshipped the Divine Mother in practices of unrivaled beauty and grace.

◆Total cost of the Bali Quest is $3500 US. ($3000 for Early Reg. Before Sept 1.) This includes transfers to the beautiful **Nefatari Villas of Ubud,** double and quad villa occupancy in traditional Balinese settings, Balinese cuisine, some planned excursions, and Bali Quest training tuition.

◆**Register Here**: https:// sondraray.com/ programs-quests/

◆ Only 25 Spaces available.

◆Email <contact@sondraray.com> for info and program.

225

NOTES

NOTES

NOTES

Printed in Great Britain
by Amazon

40063345R00142